Russia and China
Anatomy of a Partnership

edited by Aldo Ferrari
and Eleonora Tafuro Ambrosetti

© 2019 Ledizioni LediPublishing
Via Alamanni, 11 – 20141 Milano – Italy
www.ledizioni.it
info@ledizioni.it

Russia and China. Anatomy of a Partnership
Edited by Aldo Ferrari and Eleonora Tafuro Ambrosetti
First edition: May 2019

The opinions expressed herein are strictly personal and do not necessarily reflect the position of ISPI.

Print ISBN 9788867059799
ePub ISBN   9788867059805
Pdf ISBN   9788867059812
DOI   10.14672/67059799

ISPI. Via Clerici, 5
20121, Milan
www.ispionline.it

Catalogue and reprints information: www.ledizioni.it

Table of Contents

Introduction 7
Paolo Magri

1. Russia and China:
   Countering the Dominance of the West 13
   Aldo Ferrari, Eleonora Tafuro Ambrosetti

2. The Asymmetrical Russia-China Axis:
   An Overview 37
   Alexander Gabuev, Vita Spivak

3. Russia and China:
   An Enhanced Security Cooperation 61
   Alessandro Arduino

4. Russia and China:
   The Progressive Building of a Major Trading Bloc 87
   Alessia Amighini

5. The Sino-Russian Challenge
   to the US Dollar Hegemony 109
   Vasilii Nosov

Policy Recommendations for the EU 133
Aldo Ferrari, Eleonora Tafuro Ambrosetti

The Authors 139

Introduction

There was a time when many people – most Westerners, at least – took for granted the liberal US-championed world order as famously depicted, for instance, by Francis Fukuyama in *The End of History and the Last Man*. Fukuyama argued that with the collapse of the Soviet Union the last ideological alternative to liberalism had been eliminated, and even in nominally Communist states like China political and economic reform was heading in a liberal direction. As Fukuyama and others put it: the end of history.

That time was not so long ago, but today it seems a lost age. Our world nowadays tends rather to resemble another famous description, that of the British historian Niall Ferguson. Unlike Fukuyama, he saw the demise of the USSR as the starting point of the "Descent of the West" and the inevitable rise of China to economic hegemony. In the 2019 ISPI report ("The End of a World. The Decline of the Liberal Order"), we analysed the far-reaching consequences of these developments on the resilience of the international system, on multilateral organisations, and even on the institutional structure of individual states.

Where does Eurasia fit in this picture? The decline of the West now appears as commonplace, while the rise of Eurasia as an increasingly important hub of political and economic power is attracting more and more attention worldwide. That, certainly, is the story which Russia and China have been telling for years. Of course, opinions on such developments often differ according to one's viewpoint. But notwithstanding such differences, few would discount China's impressive economic performance or the political influence of a resurgent Russia in the international arena; and even fewer would disagree that the two countries' worsening clashes with the West are drawing Beijing and Moscow closer together, potentially challenging the world liberal order and especially its American leader.

The Shanghai Cooperation Organisation (SCO) may well be the most visible sign of a "Eurasian shift" in global alliances, even if its effectiveness may have been diluted by its recent enlargement and by differences in the interests of its two founding members, Russia and China. But Sino-Russian cooperation does not stop there: economic and military cooperation (from the fight against terrorism within the SCO to joint military exercises, such as Vostok-2018 last September) go hand in hand with a convergence of political attitudes, maybe even of values to some extent. This ISPI Report tackles every aspect of what appears to be a steadily building alliance between Moscow and Beijing, but it also warns of the growing asymmetries characterising it. These asymmetries are present across the board but are especially visible in the economic field: Russia's GDP is nowadays no bigger than that of Guangdong province, and its defence spending is just one-third of China's. It is hard not to see who has the upper hand in this relationship.

In the opening chapter, Ferrari and Tafuro Ambrosetti get to the heart of what has been considered a Sino-Russian challenge to the global liberal order. First, they recommend the term "revisionism" (in a neutral sense) to describe Russian and Chinese foreign policies since the early 2000s: the term refers to both countries' willingness to question "the rules of the game", that is, the rules of the US-backed liberal order. Second, they examine the Sino-Russian challenge to Western values, identifying three main ideas most warmly supported by Beijing and Moscow: multipolarity, their right to adopt "homegrown" values as opposed to "universal" ones, and sovereign stability in the face of Western interference. Third, they look at the geopolitical shifts entailed by a "post-Western world order" which Russia, in particular, loudly advocates but which also involves risks for Moscow from the increasingly asymmetrical relation with a stronger and richer Beijing.

Gabuev and Spivak go over the ups and downs of Sino-Russian relations, showing how their political centre of gravity has shifted over the years. They argue that it was only after the global financial crisis of 2008 that Moscow came to realise the need to engage with its "giant neighbour". Russia may have felt superior to China throughout the 20th century; but things changed dramatically after the millennium, and in particular after 2014 when heightened tension with the West over the Ukrainian crisis forced Russia to adapt to the role of China's junior partner.

Still, Russia and China seem content with this asymmetrical model of cooperation, at least for the present, as we see from Arduino's study of the enhanced military and security cooperation between them. Arduino reviews the range of security risks in Eurasia associated with the land segment of China's Belt and Road Initiative and investigates the ways in which Russia can help to mitigate those risks, partly through multilateral cooperation within the SCO and partly by means of its private security companies. Joint anti-terrorist activities are informed by the two countries' views on the nature and implications of the terrorist threat: while the US seems to view terrorism primarily as a threat from outside, Russia and China see terrorism, separatism, and religious extremism as a *domestic* source of dangers to national unity.

Political will in Moscow and Beijing also helped to drive a gradual rise in economic cooperation between Russia and China and to improve coordination between their regional integration projects. Amighini analyses their bilateral trade relationship and the structure of this trade throughout the 1990s and explains how, in the next decade, the two countries overcame the difficulties they had experienced in building stronger trade, investment, and energy relations. The author claims that the recent free trade agreement between the Russian-led

Eurasian Economic Union and China's Belt and Road Initiative (EAEU-China FTA) is a challenge to the economic position of the EU in the world, creating as it does a large free trade zone next door to the EU in an attempt to shift the economic centre of gravity from the West to the East.

The convergence of Chinese and Russian geopolitical, economic and security interests has reached such a significant point that in many Western countries their rapprochement is perceived as posing a dramatic challenge to the established international system of neoliberal institutions, including the primacy of the US dollar in the international payments system. The 2014 agreement for a yuan-rouble foreign exchange swap between the two countries' central banks is a case in point, but Nosov's chapter warns us that Western media probably exaggerate the real impact of that agreement, and indeed of other financial and economic deals between Moscow and Beijing. As Nosov puts it, the fact that the two governments push economic cooperation despite the difficulties shows how much is at stake in their ongoing rapprochement, which brings them political advantages both domestically and internationally. However, such agreements are often just Memorandums of Understanding, a kind of non-binding, informal step before a contract is signed. In the end, though, it is up to Chinese and Russian businesses to finalise agreements based on commercial profitability, and they often fail to do so.

Are the times ripe, then, for a "Eurasian world order"? Not so fast. On the one hand the US, the EU and "the West" generally still retain a great deal of political and economic power; on the other, the relationship between China and Russia has its differences of interest; its asymmetries can only grow, and may yet impair cooperation between the two countries. All the same, while changes in the global balance of power will not – and *cannot* – happen overnight, the "Eurasian shift" is a long-term trend that will probably lead to the end of the world as we have known it. The big question facing policymakers around the globe is whether we should merely try to oppose the ending of Western ascendancy by all possible means, or should rather adapt to it, if not by embracing it then at least trying to make it as peaceful and "soft" as possible – and if so, how. A thorough understanding of this historic and multi-faceted readjustment is an obvious first step, and this should, in turn, inform decisions on matters that will keep political elites busy for the years to come.

Paolo Magri
ISPI Executive Vice President and Director

1. Russia and China: Countering the Dominance of the West

Aldo Ferrari, Eleonora Tafuro Ambrosetti

The so-called "Sino-Russian challenge to the global order"[1] should be understood in the context of a rapid deterioration in the political and institutional situation that emerged at the end of the Cold War. That world order was based on the capability and willingness of the United States to lead the international community both in peace and in war. Despite the "revolt against the West" which occurred during the twentieth century with the birth of communist states and the process of decolonisation, US hegemony has perpetuated the central position of the West in the international system. That centrality includes the ability to disseminate political, ideological, and juridical models, especially after the collapse of the USSR and the consequent disappearance of the communist ideological alternative to the Western capitalist democratic model. It is also supported by a set of international organisations largely based in or dominated by the West (United Nations, World Bank, International Monetary Fund, NATO, etc.)[2].

---

[1] On this topic see G. Rozman, *The Sino-Russian Challenge to World order. National Identities, Bilateral Relations, and East Versus West in the 2010s*, Woodrow Wilson Center, Stanford University Press, 2014.

[2] See *Introduction*, in A. Colombo, P. Magri (eds.), *The End of a World. The Decline of the Liberal Order*, Global Scenarios and Italy, ISPI Annual Report 2019, Milan, Ledizioni-ISPI, 2019, pp. 9-10.

This US-dominated international order and its political and cultural model has been increasingly challenged, and not only by the threat of Islamic radicalism, the severe 2008-2009 economic-financial crisis and the proliferation of "populisms" in many Western countries. Radical contestation by China and Russia of the Western political, economic and cultural model has posed an equally significant challenge to the primacy of the West in international affairs. Those two countries constitute the main nucleus of a growing set of states often referred to as "revisionist", very different from each other but all substantially opposed to the centuries-long hegemony of the West and the US in particular[3]. This chapter considers Russia's and China's attempts to counter Western political and normative dominance. First, it seeks to answer the crucial question of whether Russia and China are indeed revisionist powers. Second, it examines the Sino-Russian challenge to the Western liberal order in terms of values, by identifying three main ideas around which the two countries' worldviews converge most: (i) multipolarism; (ii) "homegrown" values; and (iii) sovereignty and stability. Third, it looks at the geopolitical shifts entailed by a "post-Western world order" and their possible future implications; these are then considered further in the conclusion.

Revisionism Made in China (and Russia)?

It has become common to label Russia and China "revisionist powers". As noted by the US academic analyst Jeremi Suri,

> More than anything, challenging American power has brought Russia and China together in their strategic outlook. The relationship is unequal and unstable, but the leaders of Moscow and Beijing share a common interest in weakening the United States, resisting the spread of democratic values, and exploiting the global capitalist system. They also see mutual benefits in

---

[3] See G.J. Schmitt (ed.), *Rise of the revisionists. Russia, China, and Iran*, AEI Press, Washington DC, 2018.

undermining the current international order, largely built by the United States. Their interest in selective disorder makes Russia and China, in American eyes, "revisionist" powers[4].

The application to Russia and China of the term "revisionism" can certainly be questioned. For example, Randall Schweller prefers to consider the US "the True Revisionist Power":

> Imagine another globally dominant power, say China or Russia, acted on its beliefs that: (1) its mission is to rid the world of evil by spreading what it claims are its universal values; (2) its security requires waging preventive wars; and (3) international norms, rules, and law apply to everyone else but not to itself because world order requires that it acts differently from all other states. Would we not consider that to be a revisionist power[5]?

If we use the term "revisionism" in a neutral manner there is no doubt that Moscow and Beijing are questioning the order that emerged from the dissolution of the USSR, both in local geopolitical contexts and globally. Relegated to the edge of international political life by the crisis of the 1990s, Russia has returned under Vladimir Putin to play a key international role, in particular by assertively opposing the eastward expansion of the EU and NATO, which it regards as a major threat to its national security. Clashes with the West notably include Georgia and Ukraine, which in 2003-2004 experienced the so-called "colour revolutions", seen by Moscow as regime-change manoeuvres against Russia, led by the West[6]. In particular, the

---
[4] L. Suri, *American Pressure Against Revisionist Russia and China*, ISPI Commentary, 21 December 2018.
[5] R. Schweller, *Rising Powers and Revisionism in Emerging International Orders*, Valdai Papers, no. 16, May 2015, p. 15.
[6] See the 2015 National Security Strategy, where Putin identified "foreign-sponsored regime change" as a security threat: "The main threats to state and public security are […] the activities of […] foreign and international nongovernmental organizations, and financial and economic structures, and also individuals, focused on destroying the unity and territorial integrity of the Russian Federation, destabilizing the domestic political and social situation – including through

annexation of Crimea in 2014 marked a decisive turning point in the Kremlin's foreign policy. According to Dmitri Trenin, director of the Carnegie Center in Moscow, Putin's real goal:

> [...] is not to revise parts of the post-Soviet settlement in the Black Sea area. Rather, it is to provide an alternative to the post-Cold War world order dominated by the US. While many in the US see Russia as a weak and declining country, Putin believes that the heyday of US hegemony is over[7].

Russia paid for the clash with the West over the Ukrainian issue with economic sanctions and expulsion from the G8; but its assertiveness has certainly not diminished. On the contrary, in the last few years Moscow has succeeded in imposing its influence even outside the post-Soviet space, though at the sacrifice of dwindling financial resources badly needed for domestic development. In Syria, above all, Russia has effectively occupied the political space left empty by the United States. The fact that the Astana diplomatic process involves Russia, Iran and Turkey but none of the Western countries (in particular not the US) is a significant demonstration of the rapid change now taking place in the international situation.

Compared to Moscow, which from 2008 to the present has resorted to the use of military force in Georgia, Ukraine and Syria, Beijing appears so far less aggressive in its foreign policy. A possible explanation for this is a substantial difference between the two countries: over the last two decades Chinese leaders have adopted a "peaceful rise" narrative to reassure neighbouring countries that China is not a threat, and to help it achieve the aim of combining their country's impressive economic growth with a redistribution of the resulting benefits

---

inciting 'color revolutions' and destroying traditional Russian religious and moral values", http://www.ieee.es/Galerias/fichero/OtrasPublicaciones/Internacional/2016/Russian-National-Security-Strategy-31Dec2015.pdf

[7] D. Trenin, *Moscow determined to follow its own path*, Carnegie Moscow Center, 1 April 2014.

to its hundreds of millions of poor citizens[8]. To achieve its goals, then, China needs stability, peace, reliable markets and free trade; economically weak Russia, on the other hand, only stands to gain from an increase in international tension[9].

However, this aspect of Chinese foreign policy could change in the coming years. For example, John Mearsheimer – a renowned American analyst who is often critical of Western policies towards Russia – thinks it unlikely that the rise of China can be peaceful indefinitely[10]. For the moment, Beijing shows a clear desire to assert its central status in East Asia, and this is part of a plan that goes well beyond the sovereignty of a few little islands in the South China Sea: like Russia, China also intends to acquire a sphere of influence around itself, in growing opposition to US policy and interests[11]. But even this, though an important aim, is a limited one. The real crux of the matter is that Moscow and Beijing dispute the legitimacy of the unipolar order established after the collapse of the USSR, an international system dominated by the single state with the greatest political, economic and military power.

Both Russia and China can, therefore, be considered revisionist powers because they advocate a transformation of the international order so as to escape a much-resented inferiority to the United States. At the same time, as Richard Sakwa observes, Moscow and Beijing do not challenge the fundamental rules of the international legal system, but essentially want to gain greater importance within it[12]. Michael J. Mazarr also considers Russia and China the main dissenters from the

---

[8] E. Pan, *The Promise and Pitfalls of China's 'Peaceful Rise'*, Council on Foreign Relations (CFR), 2006.
[9] See M. Lubina, *Russia and China. A political marriage of convenience*, Barbara Budrich Publishers, Opladen - Berlin - Toronto, 2017, p. 48.
[10] See J.J. Mearsheimer, The *Tragedy of Great Powers Politics*, London, Norton, 2014, pp. 340-411.
[11] See Th. Wright, *China and Russia vs. America: Great-power revisionism is back*, Brookings, 27 April 2015.
[12] See R. Sakwa, *Russia against the Rest. The post-cold war crisis of world order*, Cambridge University Press, Cambridge, 2017, pp. 288-289.

international system dominated by the United States; they both support changes to make the system less imperialist and more pluralistic[13]. The idea that Russia and China intend to subvert the international order, in particular by promoting their own authoritarian political systems ("autocracy promotion"), does not seem to correspond to reality[14].

China and Russia, then, act as revisionist powers only when they feel their interests are threatened or slighted, but act as *status quo* powers in forums where they occupy a powerful position, such as the United Nations Security Council (UNSC), where Russia and China have a veto. They can therefore be described as [...] "soft revisionist – they revise the current International system, but softly, without creating a block or military alliance"[15]. The question of whether China and Russia are forming a *normative* alliance is examined in the next section.

A Normative Convergence?

China and Russia feature prominently in the latest United States Intelligence Community Worldwide Threat Assessment (WTA). The WTA accuses both countries of endangering US national security at many levels, from cybersecurity to arms control – including space warfare. The WTA also highlights another type of challenge Russia and China are posing to the US: a *normative* challenge to the US-championed global liberal order:

> China and Russia are more aligned than at any point since the mid-1950s, and the relationship is likely to strengthen in the coming year as some of their interests and threat perceptions converge, particularly regarding perceived US unilateralism and interventionism and Western promotion of democratic values

---

[13] See M.J. Mazarr, "The Once and Future Order: What comes after Hegemony?", *Foreign Affairs*, vol. 96, no. 1, January/February 2017, p. 25.
[14] See K. Yakouchyk, "Beyond Autocracy Promotion: A review", *Political Studies Review*, 2018, pp. 1-14.
[15] M. Lubina (2017), p. 74.

and human rights. [...] As China and Russia seek to expand their global influence, they are eroding once well-established security norms and increasing the risk of regional conflicts, particularly in the Middle East and East Asia[16].

This quote exposes US fears of an increasing alignment of values between two of the countries that Washington perceives as most dangerous to its interests and its global role. That alignment is not a recent development: the years following the end of the Cold War already showed the first signs of a Sino-Russian convergence towards the common goal of a "new international order". As Anderson claims: "within a year of the Soviet Union's collapse in 1991, Russia began to court China anew. By 1996, the two countries had forged an apparently fresh relationship – a so-called strategic partnership – based on shared domestic and international concerns. [...] Beijing and Moscow claim this emerging partnership as the foundation for a new security mechanism in the Asia-Pacific region and, eventually, a new international order"[17].

The WTA quote also hints at the reasons why this alignment is proceeding faster now: today more than ever the US is an enemy for both China and Russia. Until recently, the two countries differed in their background and history of engagement with the US, making their perceptions of risk – especially the risk of western interference in their domestic affairs – different as well. As already mentioned earlier in this chapter, the US has long embodied Russia's "enemy other"; since the start of the Cold War, first the USSR and then the Russian Federation viewed the US with a mix of fear and distrust. Since the colour revolutions, and particularly after the Ukraine crisis in 2013, anxiety and paranoia have characterised perceptions of each other on

---

[16] D.R. Coats, "Worldwide Threat Assessment of the US Intelligence Community", Statement for the record, 29 January 2019, p. 4.
[17] J. Anderson, *The Limits of Sino-Russian Strategic Partnership*, New York, Routledge, 2013, p. 7.

both sides[18]. It is evident from both governments' foreign policy statements, as well as opinion polls[19], that "anxiety and paranoia" are still dominant, reducing the space for compromise and leading towards greater competition and conflict. Russia's relation with the EU is more complex: historically, Europe has been of paramount importance to Russia's identity-formation process, and this is still true today, though Moscow has very different attitudes towards different EU member states. Wishnick explains well the interplay of different layers of identity as they affect Russia's foreign policy:

> For Russia, elaborating its own unique Euro-Asian identity is crucial to its claim to global rather than regional status, though complicated by interactions with and reactions to multiple "Others". [...] While differences with Asian – especially Chinese – "Others" reinforces Russia's sense of self as European [...], it is tensions with "Others" in the West and pressure by the US and EU that drive Russia to accentuate its Asian identity and engage with its neighbours in Asia, especially China[20].

China, on the other hand, has not had the same "obsession" with competing with the West. Its traditional sense of identity did not have the West as a historical referent[21]. But China's

---

[18] N.R. Smith, "The re-emergence of a 'mirror image' in West-Russia relations?", *International Politics*, 2017, doi:10.1057/s41311-017-0095-z.

[19] There is widespread distrust among Russians about Americans: According to a 2018 Levada poll, two out of three Russians say that their country has enemies, of which the US is the biggest adversary. ВРАГИ РОССИИ https://www.levada.ru/2018/01/10/vragi-rossii/. The same applies to the US too, where Americans' views of Russia have reached the most negative level since the fall of the Soviet Union, according to a Gallup survey published in February 2019, https://news.gallup.com/poll/247100/majority-americans-consider-russia-critical-threat.aspx?utm_source=twitter&utm_medium=o_social&utm_term=&utm_content=&utm_campaign

[20] E. Wishnick, "In search of the 'Other' in Asia: Russia – China relations revisited", *The Pacific Review*, July 2016, p. 2.

[21] J.L. Wilson, "Russia and China Respond to Soft Power: Interpretation and Readaptation of a Western Construct", *Politics*, 2015, vol. 35, nn. 3-4, pp. 287-300, p. 288.

national rebirth after the colonial era's "one hundred years of national humiliation" (1842-1949) has entailed a rebirth of traditional Sinocentrism and, therefore, an inevitable opposition to Western hegemony and US unipolarism[22]. Due to Trump's aggressive stance on China and the consequences of the US-China trade war, Beijing's feeling of resentment and distrust toward the US has grown. In Gabuev's words, "shortsighted US policies are pushing Russia and China closer together"[23].

The exact nature of this "coming together" is contested. Some analysts portray the relationship between Russia and China as a mere "political marriage of convenience"[24] or even "an axis of convenience"[25], arguing that China and Russia have not overcome all their differences – especially when it comes to geopolitical ambitions, as the next section shows: China is still an "uncomfortable neighbor", and its economic and political rise is still worrisome for Russia. Beijing's presence in the Far East of Russia still prompts fears in Moscow as much as in Irkutsk; more so, indeed, as Russia, the world's most spacious country, has a population only 10% of China's[26]. Russia's fear of China's economic dominance in Central Asia, where Moscow tries to maintain its influence and its privileged role, has now become a well-established fact.

Yet it would be a mistake to dismiss the "values" aspect of the relationship, which seems to have evolved into a much closer partnership informed by a shared worldview. Russia and China have been moving into a closer alignment around some common values for some years now. "Alliance" is probably not the best term for the real dynamics of this Russo-Chinese alignment

---

[22] See M. Lubina (2017), pp. 42-44.
[23] A. Gabuev, "Why Russia and China Are Strengthening Security Ties", *Foreign Affairs*, 24 September 2018. See also G. Rozman, "Asia for the Asians: Why Chinese-Russian Friendship Is Here To Stay", *Foreign Affairs*, 29 October 2014.
[24] M. Lubina (2017).
[25] B. Lo, *Axis of Convenience: Moscow, Beijing, and the New Geopolitics*, London, Royal Institute of International Affairs, 2008.
[26] https://worldpopulationreview.com/countries/russia-population/

in values; indeed it is hard to find references to a Russia-China "alliance" in official Russian discourse, and Putin openly dismissed the idea in 2014[27]. Yet since the 2001 Treaty on Good-Neighborliness, Friendship and Cooperation, Russian and Chinese leaders' statements have often stressed certain shared norms and values as guiding their partnership and their vision of the world at large.

The shared principles that Putin and Xi mention most often include equality and peaceful coexistence, mutual respect for territorial integrity, and non-interference in other countries' domestic affairs. We have grouped them under three main categories: multipolarism, homegrown values and sovereignty.

Multipolarism

Moscow supports a multipolar vision of international relations as developed primarily by Yevgeny Primakov[28] and largely focused on collaboration with Beijing[29]. The first official joint rejection of unipolarism by Russia and China dates back to 1997 when the two countries published a joint declaration at the UN General Assembly (UNGA) setting out their view of the world. The start of the declaration reads: "In a spirit of partnership, the Parties shall strive to promote the multipolarisation of the world and the establishment of a new international order"[30].

The main target of Moscow's and Beijing's criticism was – and still is – an order dominated by the US, which seeks to use talk

---

[27] "Putin, RF ne sobiraetsja sozdavat' voenno-političeskij sojuz s Kitaem" ("Putin, the Russian Federation does not seek a security-political alliance with China"), *Ria Novosti*, 17 April 2014.
[28] On Primakov, a key actor on Russian political and cultural arena, see *The unknown Primakov. Memoirs*, Publishing House TPP RF, Moscow 2016 and the article by D. Novikov, "Rycar' rossijskogo realizma" (The Knight of Russian Realism), in *Konservatizm vo vnešnej politike: XXI vek (Conservatism in foreign policy of the XXI century)*, 2017, pp. 119-132.
[29] M.L. Levin, *The Next Great Clash. China and Russia vs. The United States*, Westport-London, 2008, p. 130.
[30] "Joint Declaration on a Multipolar World and the Establishment of a New International Order", adopted in Moscow on 23 April 1997.

of human rights and democracy as a way of imposing its interests. The way in which Russia and China see the Responsibility to Protect (R2P) principle as, essentially, "an abuse of humanitarian language and a smokescreen in the pursuit of geopolitical interests"[31] – is a case in point[32]. Russia and China see multipolarism as the only possible form of resistance to the perceived liberal hegemony of the West. The alternative they put forward is a world where the US does not hold a hegemonic position but has to grapple with other centers of power whose interests and values deserve equal recognition.

The two countries' histories, as well as their current perceptions of their roles in today's international relations, help to explain their endorsement of multipolarism. Both have an imperial past; both seek recognition for their historic role as great powers and centers of civilisation. The "glorious past" informs today's self-image. Currently, Russia and China can be considered (re)emerging or rising powers, i.e. states that (i) hold a considerable amount of power; (ii) see themselves as on the rise in international relations; and (iii) look at the Western-dominated system from the outside[33].

The drive is for both political and economic multipolarism. Politically, Russia and China defend their right to participate in global governance on an equal footing with the US, and to maintain a non-liberal domestic political system free from

---

[31] X. Kurowska, "Multipolarity as resistance to liberal norms: Russia's position on responsibility to protect", *Conflict, Security & Development*, vol. 14, no. 4, 2014, pp. 489-508, cit. p. 489.

[32] However, Snetkov and Lanteigne claim that the distance between the two states on "acceptable" policies toward international intervention in civil conflicts is increasing, with Russia assuming the role of the "loud dissenter" in global dialogues on humanitarian intervention and China opting for the position of a "cautious partner". See A. Snetkov, M. Lanteigne, "The Loud Dissenter and its Cautious Partner – Russia, China, global governance and humanitarian intervention", *International Relations of the Asia-Pacific*, vol. 15, no. 1, 1 January 2015, pp. 113-146.

[33] A. Hurrell, "Hegemony, liberalism and global order: what space for would-be great powers?", *International Affairs*, vol. 82, no. 1, 2006, pp. 1-19.

Western interference. Economically, Russia and China aim to expand the role of non-Western states in the main international financial institutions (particularly the World Bank and the IMF), and to extend the use of local currencies in international trade[34]. Both Putin and Xi have often called for reform of the system of global economic governance, and each sees the US as a major constraint on his country's ability to achieve its legitimate position in the contemporary world economic order[35].

To increase their influence, Russia and China actively participate in multilateral organisations, especially the "exclusive clubs" which bring together leading states but with a low level of institutionalisation that might limit state sovereignty and interfere in member countries' domestic affairs. The UN is a case in point: as previously mentioned, both countries are permanent members of the UNSC and show a general alignment of interests and foreign policy goals compared to the other three members, as can be seen from voting patterns in the UNSC (especially before the Syria crisis)[36]. Both stress the importance of the UN as the main legitimate forum for practising multilateralism, prioritising development and dialogue over sanctions, and conducting their struggle against the Western interference in their domestic affairs which they perceive as inherent in talk of human rights.

Russia's 2006 Foreign Policy Review calls the UN "the universal forum that has been given unique legitimacy, [...] and the main element of contemporary multilateral diplomacy"[37]. On 28 September 2015, just a few days before Russia's military intervention in Syria, Putin made a speech in the UNGA in

---

[34] See chapter 4 in this volume.
[35] E. Wishnick (2016), p. 4.
[36] P. Ferdinand, *The positions of Russia and China at the UN Security Council in the light of recent crisis*, Briefing Paper, EU Parliament Directorate-General for External Policies of the Union, Directorate B, Policy Department, 2013.
[37] Russian MFA, A Survey Of Russian Federation Foreign Policy, 2006, http://archive.mid.ru//brp_4.nsf/e78a48070f128a7b43256999005bcbb3/89a30b3a6b-65b4f2c32572d700292f74?OpenDocument

which he called for US hegemony to give way to a world policed by the UN – in which Russia, as a member of the Security Council, would play one of the leading roles. Though Putin emphasised the threat of further destabilisation in Syria and more gains by the Islamic State (IS), he also argued that this gloomy scenario could be avoided through coordinated international action under the aegis of the UN with political mediation by Russia[38].

China has also become more active in the UN. According to one prominent analyst, after years of low-profile activity at the UNGA China has stepped up its presence and is now filling a "Trump-sized vacuum"; taking advantage of US disengagement, China's long term goal appears to be to legitimise, through the UN, a vision of international development and cooperation rivalling the US-led global order[39]. It is noteworthy that China's financial contribution is now the second largest, and its contribution to peacekeeping operations, while less than is often supposed (some 2,350 blue helmets), could increase greatly[40].

Emphasis on local homegrown values

Chinese and Russian opposition to the West's "normative imperialism" is well-documented. Their view is that no country should be forced to adopt values and standards that are alien to its culture and historical experience. Two telling examples of their "local interpretation" of basic liberal values are the concepts of "managed democracy"[41] (referring to Russia's own

---

[38] V. Putin, 70th session of the UN General Assembly, 28 September 2015, http://en.kremlin.ru/events/president/news/50385
[39] R. Gowan, "China fills a Trump-sized vacuum at the UN", *Politico*, 24 September 2018.
[40] F. Godement, *The United Nations of China: A vision of the world order*, European Council on Foreign Relations (ECFR), 2018.
[41] Experts close to the Kremlin introduced the concept of "managed democracy" to describe Putin's emphasis on building a strong state and economic reforms over democratic ones in the first years of his mandate. See M. Lipman,

political path) and China's "market socialism"[42] – disproving the positive correlation between economic growth and political liberalisation long assumed by the liberal school of thought[43].

Russia aims to offer an alternative to the morally decadent West by depicting itself as a defender of conservative (anti-liberal) value[44]. While Russians' behavior seems not to differ greatly from that of Western Europeans (judging by rates of divorce, church attendance and abortion[45]), the Kremlin uses a conservative narrative both domestically and internationally. Western secularism, changes in the idea of the "traditional family" and defense of sexual minorities' rights are perceived as worrisome signs of Europe's detachment from its Christian roots. Russia's stress on conservatism and Christianity is a key element in Putin's attraction to right-wing conservatives and even populists both in Europe and in the US[46]. In France, for instance, the leader of the Front National, Marine Le Pen, has called him "a true patriot and defender of European values"[47].

M. McFaul, "Managed Democracy" in "Russia: Putin and the Press", *Harvard International Journal of Press/Politics*, vol. 6, no. 3, 2001, pp. 116-127; and A.P. Tsygankov, *The Strong State in Russia: Development and Crisis*, Oxford, Oxford University Press, 2014.

[42] A system predominantly based on public ownership and state-owned enterprises within a market economy. See S.G. Karsten, "China's Approach to Social Market Economics: The Chinese Variant of Market Socialism Seeks to Escape from the Difficulties of Central Command Planning", *The American Journal of Economics and Sociology*, vol. 47, no. 2, April 1988, pp. 129-148.

[43] G. O'Donnell, P.C. Schmitter, and L. Whitehead, *Transitions from Authoritarian Rule*, Baltimore, JHU Press, 1986.

[44] E. Tafuro Ambrosetti, *Fatal Attraction? Russia's Soft Power in Its Neighbourhood*, FRIDE Policy Brief no. 181, May 2014.

[45] See A. Ferrari, "Russia. A Conservative Society?", in Idem (ed.), *Russia 2018. Predictable Elections, Uncertain Future*, Milan, Ledizioni-ISPI, 2018.

[46] See E. Tafuro Ambrosetti, "National-Populism in Russia: Ticking All the Boxes?", in A. Martinelli (ed.), *When Populism Meets Nationalism*, Milano, Ledizioni-ISPI, 2018.

[47] A. Polyakova, "Strange Bedfellows: Putin and Europe's Far Right", *World Affairs*, vol. 177, no. 3, September/October 2014, pp. 36-40.

In China there has been a revival of the traditional understanding of morality based on Confucian values[48]. According to Lukin, Confucianism differs sharply from traditional Christianity and shaped a pragmatic culture where "monotheistic religions and their absolute morality never gained wide currency"; in any case, China's disagreement with Western individualism's understanding of human rights, which prioritises individual rights over societal and state goals, made it hard for China to find common ground with the West in the field of values[49].

China and Russia also have similar views on soft power, which is seen as deriving from state initiatives rather than from a free and active civil society[50]. According to Wilson, this similarity of views is based on the countries' common legacy of a Communist experience, which still affects their behaviour and sense of national identity today[51]. Rozman explains that Putin and Xi champion similar ideologies ("pride in the socialist era") to justify their rule and their opposition to US hegemonism[52]. As with multipolarism (above), opposition by Russia and China to Western ideas helps to draw them closer in defense of homegrown values. This applies also to their understanding of sovereignty and stability, which is examined in the next section.

Sovereignty and political stability

Sovereignty and stability have come to occupy a prominent role in the political narratives used by Russia and China both

---

[48] T. Lodén, *Confucius Returns – The Resurgence of Traditional Culture in China*, Institute for Security and Development Policy; J. Page, "Why China Is Turning Back to Confucius", *Wall Street Journal*, 20 September 2015.

[49] A. Lukin, "Russia, China, and the Emerging Greater Eurasia", in G. Rozman, S. Radchenko, *International Relations and Asia's Northern Tier*, Washington DC, Asan-Palgrave Macmillan Series, 2018, pp. 79-80.

[50] J. Nye, "What China and Russia Don't Get About Soft Power", *Foreign Policy*, 29 April 2013; J.L. Wilson, "Russia and China Respond to Soft Power: Interpretation and Re-adaptation of a Western Construct", *Politics*, 28 April 2015.

[51] J.L. Wilson (2015), p. 287.

[52] G. Rozman, "Asia for the Asians: Why Chinese-Russian Friendship Is Here To Stay"…, cit.

domestically and internationally. As Odgaard says, China and Russia regard "absolute sovereignty" as the basis of international legitimacy; meanwhile their "common communist authoritarian legacy makes them associate stability with authoritarian control rather than democratic participation"[53]. In Russia, "stability" is often opposed to the chaos experienced by the country in the 1990s after the fall of the USSR.

Several factors explain the two countries' position on sovereignty and stability. First, both have non-liberal political systems with shrinking space for dissent, and they regard human rights essentially as a domestic issue, not to be picked on by the West as a way of interfering in their affairs[54]. Second, both countries have faced or still face grave dangers of separatism and international terrorism. China perceives ethnically-based terrorism and separatism among Uyghurs as a "core national security interest" affecting its sovereignty, unity, and territorial integrity[55]. Moscow's memories of the Chechen wars are still fresh, and concerns over terrorism in the North Caucasus have not disappeared; Russia also fears possible contagion spreading from the Middle East to its own territory, especially after the "Arab Spring" revolutions, which were not officially opposed by the Kremlin at first but later perceived as dangerous, Western-backed revolts threatening legitimate governments and regional stability[56].

Russia's adherence to the principles of sovereignty and non-interference was put to the test by Moscow's annexation of Crimea and support for rebels in Eastern Ukraine, initially denied by the Kremlin[57]. China did not join the Western

---

[53] L. Odgaard, "Beijing's Quest for Stability in its Neighborhood: China's Relations with Russia in Central Asia", *Asian Security*, vol. 13, no. 1, pp. 41-58, 2017, cit. p. 51.
[54] See P.J. Bolt, S.N. Cross, *China, Russia, and Twenty-First Century Global Geopolitics*, Oxford, Oxford University Press, 2018, p. 44.
[55] *Ibid.*, p. 46.
[56] Y. Nikitina, "The 'Color Revolutions' and 'Arab Spring' in Russian Official Discourse", *Connections*, vol. 14, no. 1, Winter 2014, pp. 87-104.
[57] S. Walker, "Putin admits Russian military presence in Ukraine for first time",

bloc in condemning Russia's actions in Ukraine, still less in imposing sanctions, which were criticised in a joint Sino-Russian statement on 8 May 2015[58]. On the contrary, Beijing defended Moscow's decision as the only possible outcome of a Western provocation: the West had interfered in the domestic affairs of Ukraine first, jeopardising the stability of the whole region. In Lukin's words, "although Russian countermeasures are considered in Beijing to be extreme and not fully conducive to stability, on the whole the Russian position is met with understanding and even approval"[59]. Though we cannot know how far China's approval is genuine, this is clearly a situation in which Beijing has deliberately decided not to criticise Moscow's actions in public.

Towards a Post-Western World?

This revisionism on the part of Russia and China does not merely aim at a simple rebalancing of power among nations: it seems to adumbrate a global scenario quite different from today's, one characterised primarily by a reduction of the overall preponderance of the West. This was clearly stated by Russian Foreign Minister Lavrov in an important speech in Munich on 18 February 2017:

> Humanity stands at a crossroads today. The historic era that could be called the post-Cold War order has come to an end. [...] Leaders with a sense of responsibility must now make their choice. I hope that this choice will be made in favour of building a democratic and fair world order, a post-West world order, if you will, in which each country develops its own sovereignty within the framework of international law, and will strive to balance their own national interests with those of their partners,

---

The Guardian, 17 December 2015.
[58] Joint statement by the Russian Federation and the PRC (in Russian), 8 May 2015, https://kremlin.ru/supplement/4969
[59] A. Lukin (2018), p. 82. See also chapter 2 in this volume.

with respect for each country's cultural, historical and civilisational identity[60].

Like them or not, these words do delineate a process that is indeed taking place, not least thanks to the impressive economic and political growth of many Asian countries, China above all. Russia, lacking the economic dynamism of those countries but with a strong political and cultural tradition based on its unique history, has in recent years been at the forefront of this anti-hegemonic strategy, and has indeed taken considerable risks in its duel with the West. Russian foreign policy is usually seen as aggressive; but other, less negative evaluations are also possible. Richard Sakwa, for example, interprets it as an answer to the failure of Russia's attempt to become part of a West enlarged to include its interests and sensibilities:

> Its attempts to join a transformed West had ended in failure, and instead the institutions and practices of the Historical West were reinforced. In response, Russia became one of the most active proponents of the creation of a non-West[61].

Now, however, Russia is no longer isolated but has China at its side in a strategy that should properly be considered not anti-Western, but post-Western[62]. On the one hand, this situation is positive for Moscow; but at the same time it appears extremely risky in the light of the growing disparity between the two countries[63]. Some observers see in the current unequal relationship between Russia and China a kind of reactivation of the one established in the XIII century by Prince Alexander Nevsky, who chose to surrender Russia to the Mongols of the Golden

---

[60] http://www.mid.ru/en/press_service/minister_speeches/-/asset_publisher/7OvQR5KJWVmR/content/id/2648249

[61] R. Sakwa (2017), p. 322.

[62] See *Ibid.*, pp. 279-280.

[63] See A. Ferrari, *Russian Foreign Policy between Westphalia and Greater Eurasia*, in A. Colombo, P. Magri (eds.), *Big Powers Are Back. What About Europe?*, Global Scenarios and Italy, ISPI Annual Report 2019, Milan, Ledizioni-ISPI, 2018, pp. 47-59.

Horde in order to successfully face the Teutonic Knights. On such a view, now as in the Middle Ages the East would seem less threatening to Russia than the West[64].

Regardless of the complex and problematic relationship between Moscow and Beijing, geopolitical cooperation between Russia and a number of Asian countries has been growing for some decades – and more strongly since 2012-2014. The Shanghai Cooperation Organization (SCO), a political, economic and security grouping created in 2001 as a counterweight to American influence in Asia, offered a model of geopolitical integration that was aimed essentially at the internal stability of its member states and free from the references to human rights and democracy that characterise Western international organisations. The SCO's founding members – Russia, China, Kazakhstan, Tajikistan and Uzbekistan – were joined by Pakistan and India in June 2017. Despite many observers' reservations as to its real effectiveness[65], the SCO is in fact a very important step in the institutionalisation of Russia's political, economic and security cooperation with Asian countries outside the former Soviet space. The SCO complements other organisations grouping Russia with other former Soviet countries, such as the Collective Security Treaty Organization (CSTO: Russia, Armenia, Belarus, Kazakhstan, Kyrgyzstan, and Tajikistan) and the Eurasian Economic Union (EAEU, a Common Economic Space consisting of Russia, Belarus, Kazakhstan, Armenia and Kyrgyzstan[66]). Unlike those other organisations, however, Russia does not play the lead in the SCO, but has to share it with China.

---

[64] On the so called "Nevsky Paradigm" see M. Lubina (2017), pp. 92-93.
[65] See *Ibid.*, pp. 240-245.
[66] On this topic see above all N. Vasilyeva, M. Lagutina, *The Russian Project of Eurasian Integration. Geopolitical Prospects*, Lexington Books, Lanham - Boulder - New York – London, 2016; and A. Di Gregorio, A. Angeli (eds.), *The Eurasian Economic Union and the European Union: Moving Towards a Greater Understanding*, The Hague, Eleven International Publishing, 2017.

Furthermore the EAEU, the Moscow-centered Eurasian integration project, not only has considerable internal difficulties but also has to deal with the much more dynamic Belt and Road Initiative (BRI) launched in 2013 by Beijing[67]. Moscow is trying to reconcile its project with the Chinese one, with rather limited success because of the imbalance in resources available to the two countries. On the whole, Russia tends to see the various projects in this area – EAEU, SCO and BRI – as at least potentially converging in a new political and economic community that is increasingly referred to as "Greater Eurasia", an expression coined by Vladimir Putin during the St. Petersburg economic forum in 2016.

This is how the Russian analyst Sergei Karaganov describes this project:

> The partnership or community of Greater Eurasia is, first of all, a conceptual framework that sets the direction for interaction among states on the continent. It should be committed to promoting joint economic, political, and cultural revival and development of dozens of Eurasian countries, backward or oppressed in the past, and turning Eurasia into the global economic and political center. [...] The partnership of Greater Eurasia should be based on the traditional postulates of international law and international coexistence, and rejection of all forms of universalism, supremacy of certain values over others, and one's a priori rightness or hegemony[68].

It is, in fact, a far larger development than the Kremlin's original Eurasian project, which emerges greatly diminished, especially by comparison with Beijing. Indeed, it is difficult for Moscow not to recognise, perhaps reluctantly, the historical significance of a stronger China. Alongside its outstanding

---

[67] See M. Lagutina, *Improving relations with Russia and Ukraine*, in A. Amighini (ed.), *China's Belt and Road: A Game Changer?*, Milano, Ledizioni-ISPI, 2017.

[68] S. Karaganov, *The new Cold War and the emerging Greater Eurasia*, in "Journal of Eurasian Studies", vol. 9, 2018, p. 90. On this topic see also R. Sakwa (2017), pp. 292-293; and A. Kuznetsova, *Greater Eurasia. Perceptions from Russia, the European Union, and China*, RIAC, 1 September 2017.

economic development in recent decades, China has managed, in the BRI, to set up an initiative of exceptional symbolic and practical scope: for the first time after centuries of Western economic dominance, we are witnessing a global development project coming from the East[69]. As one Russian observer has written: "Russia cannot avoid recognising China's primacy, but preserves equal rights and freedom to maneuver"[70].

This can by no means be taken for granted, given that Russia has been accustomed to thinking of itself as a great power. Faced with overwhelming Chinese dynamism, Russia must find a new geopolitical role consistent both with its ambitions and with its real potential, a role which, after the crisis with the West, seems increasingly to be finding its place not only in "Great Eurasia" but also in a post-western scenario which is also, paradoxically, favoured by current US foreign policy: for the Trump presidency is rapidly demolishing the very foundations of the international order created by the United States in previous decades. Trump is, in fact, replacing the previous liberal universalism with a vision focused primarily on great powers' national interests, something very similar to what Russia has been advocating since the days of Primakov. Trump's obsessive claim to American primacy, however startling the contrast between the countries, is part of an "ideological" context closer to Russian and Chinese positions. Under his presidency, therefore, US foreign policy, previously characterised by a running contradiction between its democratic rhetoric and the pursuit of national strategic interests, appears more compatible with the creation of the new multipolar international order championed by Russia. An order based on "conservative realism" and national sovereignty would thus seem to be replacing the Western

---

[69] It is worth noting, among other things, the complete failure of a similar project announced in 2011 by Hillary Clinton. See W. Shepard, "Afghanistan: China's 'New Silk Road' Picks Up Where Hillary Clinton's Flopped", *Forbes*, 9 September 2016; R. Sakwa (2017), pp. 292-293.

[70] D. Efremenko, "Roždenie Bol'šoj Evrazii", in *Konservatizm vo vnešnej politike: XXI vek (Conservatism in foreign policy of the XXI century)*.

one of unstoppable liberal globalisation, now upset by the political events of recent years. Of course, this attitude may be abandoned if Trump is not re-elected; but the very possibility of such a scenario would have seemed scarcely thinkable only a decade ago.

Whatever the political evolution of the US, the growth of China under Xi Jinping's strong, assertive leadership unhampered by electoral deadlines will increasingly compound the weakening of the hegemonic capabilities of the United States and of the West more generally. As Guido Samarani observes, however, it seems unlikely , at least in the medium term, that China will be able to replace the US at the centre of the global order (if indeed that is really what it wants)[71].

And this, probably, is also Russia's wish; certainly Russia has no reason to desire a scenario in which the hegemony of the United States is replaced by that of China. Moscow shares many points of view with Beijing, especially in the context of international relations, but this will probably remain the case only as long as both powers are contesting Washington's hegemony. China's establishment as a dominant power – so close geographically, and much stronger economically and demographically – would be a rather unsatisfactory prospect for Russia. It should also be remembered that, despite Russia's complicated and often conflicting relationship with the West, Russian culture and society are predominantly European, while China remains a totally "other" country. An "other" that, from the philosophical reflections of Vladimir Solov'ev in the late nineteenth century to Vladimir Sorokin's post-modern narrative today, has been an object of constant concern beneath the surface, and sometimes of open hostility[72].

---

[71] See G. Samarani, *China: The Real Challenge to Western Leadership*, in A. Colombo, P. Magri (eds.), *The End of a World. The Decline of the Liberal Order*, Global Scenarios and Italy, Annual Report 2019, Milan, Ledizioni-ISPI 2019, cit., p. 107.

[72] See T. Filimonova, "Chinese Russia: Imperial Consciousness in Vladimir Sorokin's Writing", *Region*, vol. 3, no. 2, 2014, pp. 219-244; and M. Gamsa, "Refractions of China in Russia, and of Russia in China: Ideas and Things",

Conclusion

In this chapter, we have considered the attempt by Russia and China to challenge what both countries perceive as Western liberal hegemony. We believe that the term "revisionism", used in a neutral manner, may be applied to Russian and Chinese foreign policies since the early 2000s. In recent years, we have seen increasing normative and strategic convergence between Russia and China, with important implications for the liberal order championed by the West and opposed by both countries. It is debatable whether their joint actions and normative convergence spring primarily from their "shared identity", from "short-sighted" Western policies or from unfair structures of world governance. What seems clear is that their joint efforts against what they perceive as US interference and unilateralism and the West's promotion of democratic values and human rights will continue in the near future. We cannot, therefore, call the relationship between Russia and China a mere "marriage of convenience"; nor can we ignore the fact that a perceived common threat from the West is only making that relationship closer.

For Russia, however, the relationship is not risk-free. In the new "post-Western order", which Russia is doing much to create, Moscow risks finding itself subordinate once more, but this time to China instead of the United States. This is essentially due to the economic and social stagnation that continues to prevent Russia living up to its aspirations; and it is this, at the end of the day, which makes Russia's challenge to the US-led order less substantial and less dangerous than China's.

Journal of the Economic and Social History of the Orient, vol. 60, 2017, pp. 549-584. For a broader view of the Russian-Chinese historical relationships, see above all A.V. Lukin (ed.), *Rossija i Kitaj*. Četyre veka vzajmodeistvija. Istoriia, sovremennoe sostojanie i perspektivy razvitija rossijsko-kitajskich otnošenij (*Russia and China: Four Centuries of Interaction. The History, Current State and Development Perspectives of Russian-Chinese Relations*), Moskva, Ves' Mir, 2013.

2. The Asymmetrical Russia-China Axis: An Overview

Alexander Gabuev, Vita Spivak

On September 13, 2018, the Russian President Vladimir Putin spoke at the opening of the Vostok 2018 war games, the largest military exercise held in Russia since 1981. Putin's address took a little longer than usual as there was consecutive interpretation into Mandarin Chinese. Listening to Putin's speech, shoulder to shoulder with Russian troops on the Tsugol training range in the Russian Far East, stood 3200 Chinese soldiers. Ironically, the Vostok war games were initially invented by the Russian military in the 1980s to address the threat of invasion from China during an unresolved border dispute. Almost 30 years later, forces from the People's Liberation Army were invited to take part in strategic-scale Russian military exercises for the first time in history[1].

Moscow had seen Beijing as a threat for decades, ever since the Sino-Soviet split in the 1960s. Long after the fall of the Soviet Union, the Russian elite continued its stereotypical Sinophobia: for many years China was seen as backward, underdeveloped, and generally inferior. During the 1990s the Russian elite was obsessed with building a relationship with the West and paid little or no strategic attention to China. Even at the beginning of the XXI century, China did not feature on the agenda of Moscow politicians or business leaders. Encouraged

---

[1] V. Kashin, *Vostok 2018: a New Phase of Cooperation*, Moscow Defence Brief, 2018.

by soaring commodity prices, Russian oligarchs and the CEOs of powerful SOEs were busy building pipelines to Europe and buying luxury properties in London and the south of France, while the Kremlin strove to make friends with the EU, went through a complicated relationship with the US, and tried to resuscitate Russia's great power ambitions after the fall of the Soviet Union. During the early 2000s, while Moscow was doing its best to be accepted into the prestigious club of Western powers, China's economy started its double-digit growth; but that tremendous development was at best ignored by Russia's political and business elite, and at worst a source of fear.

That elite's lack of interest in China led to a dangerous decline in Russia's ability to understand the growing Asian powerhouse[2]: by the mid-2000s there were almost no effective leaders of public opinion capable of explaining China to the Russian government, business circles, and ordinary people. Decades of perceiving China as a threat, and the elite's near-total ignorance about China's development, led to growing Sinophobia at every level of Russian society. The main fears about China focused on Beijing's supposed plans to annex depopulated, resource-rich Siberia and the Russian Far East by means of surreptitious Chinese migration into those regions.

In the end, it took the global economic crisis of 2008 to change Moscow's perception of its giant neighbour. The meltdown in the financial markets and the double-digit dip in Russian GDP had a sobering effect on the Russian leadership, and forced it to take a closer look at the growing superpower on its eastern border. When in 2012 Vladimir Putin entered the Kremlin for the third time as the president of Russia (after a temporary stint by his hand-picked successor Dmitry Medvedev), Moscow had already started to experience tensions with the West and had begun to look eastwards with greater interest. The annexation of Crimea and a direct clash with the

---

[2] A. Gabuev, "Gosudarstvo ushlo iz kitaistiki" ("The state has abandoned Sinology"), Kommersant-Vlast, no. 41, 2014.

US-led West brought Moscow closer to Beijing, but the balance of the relationship had changed: though during the XX century Russia had held the upper hand, after 2014 it was obliged to adapt to the role of China's junior partner. This chapter looks at the transformation of Russia's perceptions of China in the XXI century, and how the balance of their bilateral relationship has shifted over the years.

Russia's View of China Before 2008: A Bargaining Chip in Moscow's Relations with the West

In the early 2000s, before the 2008 economic crisis and long before the Ukraine war in 2014, the relationship between Moscow and Beijing underwent some significant developments. First, the two countries signed a border demarcation agreement in 2004 which played a pivotal role in their bilateral relationship, for the agreement diminished the mutual mistrust felt in the Kremlin and in Zhongnanhai. Delimitation of the 4200-km border was completed in 2007 and set the stage for further rapprochement between Moscow and Beijing.

Second, as commodity prices began to grow alongside China's appetite for hydrocarbons, China and Russia began to appear almost natural economic partners. China became a net importer of oil as early as 1993, but in the early 2000s its energy needs were boosted by rapid economic growth, and those years saw the first substantial deals between Russian oil giants and China. YUKOS, the energy empire of the subsequently imprisoned Mikhail Khodorkovsky, looked into building an eastward pipeline to sell Siberian oil to China and lobbied for the project at the highest levels of both governments; but it was still-born due to Khodorkovsky's arrest and then imprisonment in 2003-2004. Beijing anxiously followed the unravelling of the YUKOS affair, but later in 2004, it backed Rosneft in its endeavour to snatch control of the company's most valuable asset, Yuganskneftegaz. At that time the China National Petroleum Corporation (CNPC) was the only major oil company in the world which had no problem participating in the demolition of Khodorkovsky's empire.

Third, throughout the early 2000s, Beijing and Moscow began to share a sense of mistrust towards the West. Both China and Russia were making attempts to improve relations with the West, but neither got the welcome from the US or the EU which it expected. In the 1990s, Moscow had been disgruntled by Western criticism of its wars in Chechnya, and had vigorously protested against the US attack on Serbia, Russia's long-standing partner in the Balkans. The Kremlin witnessed with concern the growing military partnership between the US and Japan in the 1990s (Moscow and Tokyo have still not signed a peace treaty, the sticking-point being the issue of the Kuril Islands). Despite the bumpy relationship with the West in the 1990s, Vladimir Putin made several attempts to improve relations, and during his first presidential term even considered joining NATO. However, the US-led war in Iraq, the extension of NATO membership to several Central European states and overt Western sympathy with the "colour revolutions" in Ukraine and Georgia left the Kremlin utterly disillusioned about its prospects of becoming a full member of the Atlantic club.

China in the 1990s was busy rebuilding its relationship with the West after the widely-criticised Tiananmen crisis of 1989, when student protests for democracy were harshly suppressed by the People's Liberation Army in the main square in Beijing. China's foreign policy had a low profile during these years, as the country was busy with its economic transition. Hungry for Western capital and business expertise and keen to join the WTO, Beijing was eager to maintain friendly relations with the West. However, the Western sanctions on arms sales following the Tiananmen Square crisis were never lifted or eased, and meanwhile, Taiwan received an unprecedented amount of American weaponry throughout the 1990s. Western leaders repeatedly met the Dalai Lama despite Beijing's protests, and perpetually challenged China on human rights issues – something the latter perceived as interference in its domestic affairs.

Frustrated, both Beijing and Moscow grew increasingly suspicious of the West throughout the 1990s and early 2000s. Shared concerns about the West manifested themselves in the evolution of the Shanghai Cooperation Organization (SCO) that China and Russia arranged in 2001. The body was originally set up in the 1990s to solve border disputes between China and the former Soviet republics, but later evolved into an institution led by China and Russia with the idea that Beijing and Moscow could together write the rules of the game for Central Asia and then gently impose their joint will on the region's nation-states, while ridding it of the influence of the US and other non-regional players[3].

All the same, before 2008 the relationship markedly lacked mutual trust. In 2007 Moscow, worried by Beijing's growing military muscle, informally banned sales of its most advanced weapons to China[4]. Furthermore, China was not a trading priority for Russia: even though their trade grew eightfold in the decade 1997-2007, China accounted for a relatively small proportion of all Russia's trade: only 4% at the start of that decade, and still only 8.7% at its end[5]. That eightfold growth was the result of the low initial level and the first few oil deals between Rosneft and Chinese buyers.

European countries were still the biggest customers for Russian natural resources at the beginning of the XXI century; but by the mid-2000s tension between the West and Russia was starting to grow, and during the Russia-Ukraine gas dispute in 2005-2006 Europeans started to look elsewhere for suppliers other than Gazprom; Moscow then played the "China card" to put pressure on Brussels. In 2006, Vladimir Putin visited Beijing, and a Memorandum of Understanding (MOU) was signed between Gazprom and CNPC. The MOU included a

---

[3] A. Gabuev, *Bigger, Not Better: Russia Makes the SCO a Useless Club*, Carnegie Moscow Center, 2017.
[4] C. Clover, "Russia resumes advanced weapons sales to China", *Financial Times*, 3 November 2016.
[5] *Bilateral Trade between Russian Federation and China*, Trade Map, 2018.

plan to build two gas pipelines with a combined capacity of 68bcm/year from Siberia straight to China. The project outlined in the MOU envisaged a pipeline not only from Eastern Siberia but also from Western Siberia, the EU's primary source of gas. European countries read Moscow's signal correctly and were quick to renew their Gazprom gas contracts. The China card had served its purpose, and Gazprom's plans to expand cooperation with CNPC receded into the background once again, to Beijing's great frustration.

Russia's View of China After 2008: An Increasingly Important Partner

China was far from a priority for the Russian leadership for decades, but the 2008 global financial crisis was a cold shower to the Kremlin. Most Western countries experienced serious financial trouble; Russian GDP dropped by 7.8%[6], but the Chinese economy thrived. China's GDP grew by 9.6% in 2008, and by 2010 was back into double-digit growth at 10.6%. This impressive growth was secured by Beijing's US$585 billion monetary stimulus in the form of increased government capital spending on infrastructure. Nonetheless, the Kremlin was clearly impressed.

Suffering from the economic recession and the rapidly falling demand for commodities, Russian companies had no other choice but to seek finance in China: there were no available alternatives in the West, which was busy dealing with its own economic problems. Beijing was aware of Moscow's despair, and leveraged it skilfully: at the time, the Russian energy giants Rosneft and Transneft were struggling with the East Siberia – Pacific Ocean (ESPO) pipeline and urgently needed cash to finish the project. Despite existing worries about restricting themselves a single customer in the East, Rosneft and Transneft signed a contract with CNPC in 2009 which committed them

---

[6] World Bank, GDP Growth (annual %), electronic database, 2017.

to build a direct pipeline to China. In exchange, the China Development Bank provided them with a US$25 billion loan backed by a 20-year oil supply contract (15 million tons a year)[7]. Then in 2011, China continued to exploit its new predominance in the bilateral relationship[8]: Beijing squeezed out an additional discount for the oil by threatening to drop the project for good and leave Rosneft with an almost-completed one-way oil pipeline and a huge debt. By that time, Beijing had already provided itself with alternatives to the ESPO pipeline: it could easily replace Russian oil exports with the supplies from Kazakhstan through the newly constructed Atasu-Alashankou pipeline commissioned in 2006.

Despite Beijing's hard bargaining position, many Russian companies followed Rosneft and Transneft and went seeking finance in the Chinese market. UC Rusal, a Russian aluminium giant, conducted an IPO on the Hong Kong Stock Exchange. Rusal's investors were not thrilled by the company's decision, but the deal displayed a clear political message within Russia and to the world at large: Russian companies had alternatives to the American and European capital markets. Furthermore, bilateral trade began to grow steadily after 2009: soon China surpassed Germany and the Netherlands, in 2010 becoming Russia's biggest trading partner (among nation-states, not counting the EU as a whole)[9]. China's top ten trading partners, on the other hand, still do not include Russia.

Though economic interests were the main driving force behind Russia's "discovery" of China, geopolitical factors were also starting to bring Moscow and Beijing closer together. In 2009 Russia hosted Brazilian, Indian, and Chinese leaders for the first ever BRIC summit, a grouping based on a concept[10]

---

[7] R. Paxton, V. Soldatkin, "China lends Russia $25 billion to get 20 years of oil", *Reuters*, 2009.
[8] K. Melnikov, A. Gabuev, and A. Gudkov, "Kitai visoko utsenil rossiskuyu neft" ("China highly depreciated the Russian oil"), *Kommersant*, 28 February 2012.
[9] *Russian Federation exports and imports*, Trade Map, 2018.
[10] J. O'Neil, *Building Better Global Economics BRICs*, Goldman Sachs, Global

coined by the Goldman Sachs economist Jim O'Neil back in 2001. South Africa joined the group in 2010, changing its name to BRICS; membership since then has been unchanged.

But in geopolitical terms, too, Beijing turned out to be a difficult partner for Moscow. By the end of the 2000s, the SCO was becoming increasingly Beijing-centred due to the growth of China's economy and international standing. Moscow was forced to come to terms with the growing asymmetry of the two countries in all-round national power within the SCO mechanisms. After 2010, China started to actively push for the establishment of an SCO development bank and an SCO free trade zone. In Moscow's view, Chinese proposals to upgrade economic cooperation within the SCO were a ploy to turn the organisation into a tool for promoting Chinese geo-economic interests in Central Asia – at Russia's expense[11]. At that time Moscow was promoting the creation of the Eurasian Economic Union (EAEU) inspired by the EU model and designed to establish a Moscow-centred economic bloc including all the Central Asian countries except Turkmenistan. China's vision for an SCO free trade agreement ran directly counter to that project, and Moscow deployed all its diplomatic influence to thwart China's grand economic development plans for the SCO; in the end, it succeeded in throttling both the development bank and the free trade zone.

So although the China-Russia relationship began to gain momentum after the pivotal economic crisis of 2008, its path was a very bumpy one, mainly because of lingering suspicions and Russian decision-makers' lack of expert Sinologists' advice. Deeply impressed by the economic stability of the Chinese system after the global storm of the financial crisis, in 2011, President Medvedev initiated the first ever strategic assessment of Sino-Russian relations and an attempt to draw up a Russian strategy for the Asia-Pacific region in general. That (classified)

Economics, Paper no. 66, 2001.
[11] A. Gabuev, *Bigger, Not Better: Russia Makes the SCO a Useless Club...*, cit.

policy document contained an analysis of the latest development trends in Asia, and highlighted certain steps that Moscow could take to benefit from the region's dynamic growth; but the analysis was full of misconceptions, one of which was the notion that technology was a field where Russia enjoyed a competitive advantage in the Asian market. This bold and largely exaggerated conclusion probably catered to President Medvedev's obsession with Russian technological potential; it had no connection with reality[12]. At present, according to the Lowy Institute's Asia Power Index, Russian technological potential is ranked tenth in East Asia, below Taiwan, New Zealand, and Malaysia[13]; China, on the other hand, comes second only to the United States.

Though late in the day and despite evident misconceptions, this document was Moscow's first serious comprehensive attempt to look eastwards and examine its relationship with China more closely. One year later, as Vladimir Putin started his third presidency in 2012, the Kremlin intended to pivot gradually towards Asia and upgrade its partnerships in the region step by step; but the war in Ukraine, the annexation of Crimea and the stagnation of the Russian economy exacerbated by Western sanctions forced Moscow to seek closer cooperation with China with an additional urgency that further embedded the existing asymmetry in the bilateral relationship.

---

[12] This suggestion is based on a series of over fifty semi-structured interviews with Russian officials, businessmen, and experts conducted in 2014-2017 by Alexander Gabuev as part of ongoing research on Russia-China relations within the Russia in the Asia Pacific Program of the Carnegie Moscow Center. Most of the interviewees asked for anonymity as they were not authorised to speak about Sino-Russian relations. To save space and avoid burdening the reader with links to anonymous interviews, no more footnotes will reference these interviews unless needed.

[13] Lowy Institute, *Asia Power Index 2018*, 2018, https://power.lowyinstitute.org/

Russia's View of China Post-2014: A Strategic Partner

Political turmoil in Kiev, the annexation of Crimea, and the war in Eastern Ukraine led to the most serious clash between Moscow and the West since the collapse of the Soviet Union. As the first round of Western sanctions hit in 2014, the Kremlin started to realise its growing vulnerability in the unfolding conflict with the West, due to its almost total dependence on Europe and America for Russian hydrocarbon sales, access to technological know-how, and low-interest loans. If it was to survive this confrontation with the West, Moscow urgently needed a strong partner; and China, a major economic power which did not appear intent on joining in the international condemnation of Russia, seemed the only reasonable candidate. Besides, China had for years experienced its own tensions with the West over its status as a market economy, human rights, Taiwan, etc.

In 2014, the Russian government conducted a second round of due diligence about China. This time, many official agencies, experts, and business leaders took part in the risk assessment process. The urgency of the external climate made Moscow take a more realistic view of its largest eastern neighbour, which by that time was well on the way to becoming the biggest economy in the world. The Kremlin's 2014 analysis concluded that China had become fundamentally more powerful than Russia in almost all aspects, contradicting the naïve views of 2011 about Russian technological superiority to China and other Asian countries. Another important point was that despite its growing strength China posed no threat to Russia, at least in the short term. The Kremlin understood that, unlike Washington, Beijing would not pressure Moscow to adopt its own world view and set of values. Also, Moscow's long-standing anxieties about China's "demographic threat" to Siberia and the Russian Far East, the modernisation of its armed forces and its ambitions in Central Asia were significantly re-evaluated and almost eliminated in the 2014 results. These two important conclusions about China's strengths and the potential challenges and benefits of its rise underpinned Moscow's rapid pivot to China after the first round of Western sanctions.

Even though the Russian leadership's decision in principle to turn to China after the geopolitical earthquake of 2014 was better informed than before, it carried a set of inflated expectations about a partner that had been treated with mistrust and neglect for decades. The Russian leadership expected that as soon as China saw the Kremlin eager to enhance cooperation, it would jump in and replace the West as Russia's main energy customer, lender, and source of technology. On top of that, Moscow had big hopes of Chinese infrastructure investments, now vastly expanded under the Belt and Road Initiative announced in 2013.

The first round of Western sanctions was imposed in March 2014; less than two months later Vladimir Putin travelled to Shanghai and together with the Chinese leader Xi Jinping oversaw the signing of over 30 agreements and contracts. The US$400 billion Power of Siberia gas pipeline deal signed by Gazprom and CNPC was the major event of the bilateral summit. The project was a significant victory for Moscow in its growing confrontation with the West.

Nevertheless, many of the agreements signed in Shanghai were just MOUs without specific details. A year later, when the oil price dropped, and the rouble with it, Russian trade with China fell by 28.6%[14]. Moreover, the Chinese partners appeared less welcoming and reliable than the Russians had anticipated: many Russian businesses had serious difficulty opening and maintaining accounts with Chinese commercial banks, which began to treat them with greater suspicion because of Western economic sanctions.

By 2016 Russia's inflated expectations for its economic rapprochement with China had almost evaporated. The Russian market was still of secondary importance to most Chinese exporters, who had developed long-standing business relations

---

[14] Trade Map, *Bilateral Trade between Russian Federation and China…*, cit.

with the West at the time when Moscow was paying no attention to the growing economic power of the People Republic. Despite the political rhetoric of the leadership about warm relations with Moscow, many big Chinese companies (especially commercial banks) had too much at stake in the West to ignore the sanctions against Russia. Besides, a gradually slowing economy, tighter capital controls, a massive anti-corruption campaign, and China's little experience and poor understanding of the Russian market were constant constraints on any deeper economic integration between Moscow and Beijing. The Russian elite's disappointment with China in 2016 led the Kremlin to the important realisation that its relationship with Beijing needed a strategic basis, a long-term vision, and a gradual approach.

Current Trends: Trade

A drop in bilateral trade with China due to the fall in commodity prices and the consequent depreciation of the rouble had a sobering effect on the Russian elite, forcing them to realise that no amount of geopolitical closeness will trump the simple market logic that drives economic engagement. Besides, the Chinese once again proved to be tough negotiators, leveraging Russia's international isolation to their advantage when it came to setting prices in oil and gas contracts.

After 2014, following government insistence on the need for export diversification, Russian food producers started actively prospecting the Chinese market, where Russian goods had been barely present earlier. Their interest was based on a belief that China would still want to import the higher-quality food that Russia could supply, mainly dairy and agricultural produce. However, as soon as Russian companies tried to enter the Chinese market, they had to face stiff competition from Western brands and the need to adjust their products to the particular tastes of Chinese customers.

As oil prices rose again after 2016, reviving bilateral trade reached US$107 billion, topping US$100 billion for the first time[15]. Moscow and Beijing hope to reach US$200 billion by 2024[16]. The Power of Siberia pipeline, which is assumed to start operating at the end of 2019, will also influence the trade volume. Moreover, Chinese companies are beginning to replace Western ones as Russia's main technology providers: despite Western suspicions of Chinese telecom companies such as Huawei and ZTE, the Russian government has been keen to buy their equipment for everyday use, suspecting that European and American IT hardware might have backdoors for Western intelligence agencies. Though many Western countries have accused Huawei and ZTE of spying for the Chinese government, to the Russian authorities, they seem at present the lesser evil.

Nevertheless, despite soaring hydrocarbon exports from Russia and booming trade in technology, the ambitious target set for 2024 by the Russian and the Chinese leadership does not seem to be achievable as things are; it will more probably be 2030 before that level of trade is reached, so long as there are no major fluctuations in the oil price.

Current Trends: Investment

China is becoming one of the leading investors in the Russian economy, but Russia still accounts for less than 0.5% of Chinese investment abroad[17]. The amount of Chinese FDI (foreign direct investment) in the Russian economy has become a much-debated topic among Russian policymakers and Chinese experts due to the difference between the Chinese and

---

[15] *Ibid.*
[16] Ministry of Economic Development of the Russian Federation, "Russia plans to boost trade with China to $200bn by 2024", 2018.
[17] Ministry of Commerce of People's Republic of China, "Statistical Bulletin of China's Outward Foreign Direct Investment", Beijing, 2018.

Russian statistics[18]. According to the Russian Central Bank, Chinese FDI in Russia amounted to US$140 billion in 2017, while China's Ministry of Commerce puts the figure more than ten times higher, at US$1.5 billion. The discrepancy boils down to accounting methods: the Chinese statistics include those investments that go to Russia through tax havens (Jersey, the Bahamas etc.), while the Central Bank of Russia only counts those which come straight from China. According to informal estimates, though, Russia had accumulated US$50 billion worth of Chinese FDI by the end of 2017, almost half of it after 2014 when Western investment shrank due to economic sanctions[19].

However Chinese FDI in Russia is calculated, it is considerably less than investment in Russia from European countries before the introduction of sanctions; and even under the sanctions regime, higher levels of FDI into Russia have come from the Netherlands, France, Switzerland, or the United Kingdom than from China.

While European FDI in Russia has always been relatively diverse, Chinese investments are notable for their particular focus on deals backed by the Russian government and involving companies associated with Putin's inner circle. Those investments are mostly by China's state-owned entities, for they have the luxury of ignoring the risks involved in working with sanctioned Russian companies and individuals. One of the most significant deals of this kind was the Silk Road Fund's purchase in 2016 of a 9.9% stake in the Yamal LNG project in the Russian Arctic for US$1.2 billion. The project belongs to the Russian energy giant Novatek, a shareholder in which is Gennady Timchenko, an old friend of Vladimir Putin and one of the first individuals to be put on OFAC's SDN list[20]. On

---

[18] V. Kashin, "Is China investing much in Russia?", Valdai Discussion Club, 9 June 2017.

[19] Author's interviews with Chinese officials conducted in October 2017 and March 2018 in Beijing.

[20] U.S. Department of the Treasury, "Specially Designated Nationals And

top of the investment by the state-owned Silk Road Fund, two Chinese state-owned banks (Export-Import Bank and China Development Bank) have provided additional finance for the project, enabling Novatek to complete the construction work with Yamal LNG. The Silk Road Fund and the Chinese energy giant Sinopec have bought two separate stakes in SIBUR, a large petrochemical company in Russia, also affiliated with Timchenko and with Kirill Shamalov, who is widely thought to be Vladimir Putin's son-in-law[21].

After 2014, Moscow began to allow Chinese investors to fund energy projects of strategic importance, which had not been the case ten years before; but that closer engagement with Chinese investors has not always gone smoothly. In 2018 Russia's leading energy giant Rosneft, headed by an old friend of Vladimir Putin, Igor Sechin, got its fingers burned in China: the private Chinese energy company CEFC undertook to acquire a 14.16% stake in Rosneft for US$9.1 billion. The deal would have been one of the biggest investments in Russia ever made by a private Chinese company, but a massive anti-corruption campaign in China spilled over from the public to the private sector: the CEFC Chairman Ye Jianming was arrested on corruption charges just months before the acquisition was about to be finalised, and it fell through.

The failed CEFC-Rosneft deal was an important landmark in high-level engagement between China and Russia in energy over the last four or five years. It had several remarkable implications: previously, Chinese state-owned investors had had no difficulty investing in projects involving sanctioned individuals from Putin's close circle (Yamal LNG, SIBUR, etc.). The CEFC case showed that, unlike state actors, a private company in China – even one supposed to have connections at the very top – could have difficulty getting finance for a deal that was "toxic" because the counterparty, a major Russian energy firm,

---

Blocked Persons List (SDN) Human Readable Lists", 15 March 2019.
[21] A. Gabuev, "China's Pivot to Putin's Friends", *Foreign Policy*, 25 June 2016.

was run by a sanctioned Russian individual from the Russian elite with strong Kremlin connections. According to the leading Chinese business publication Caixin, no international or Chinese bank was ready to provide CEFC with finance for its deal with Rosneft[22]. Secondly, after Ye's arrest, the Chinese government was at great pains to distance itself from him, and the reputations of Igor Sechin the Rosneft Ceo and of the company itself were consequently tarnished by their dealings with a company that was portrayed as a complete scam by the Chinese side. Nowadays Sechin is rumoured to be one of the biggest sceptics on engagement with China.

The scandal of Ye Jianming's arrest broke immediately before Vladimir Putin's visit to China in June 2018, but the issue was never brought up during the high-level bilateral summit at which Putin received China's highest honour, the Order of Friendship. Although on the surface the CEFC affair did not interrupt the smooth course of high-level engagement between Moscow and Beijing, it clearly showed that China and Russia still have much work to do on mutual understanding if cooperation in strategically important areas is to develop.

Current Trends: Military Cooperation

In 2007, the Russian government, cautious about China's rise and its habit of reverse-engineering military technology, stopped selling its more advanced weapons to Beijing. But after 2014, Moscow realised that China's overall military capabilities, including its home-grown military R&D, were developing so fast that there was no more than a decade's worth of competitive advantage still available for selling weaponry to its eastern neighbour. Moreover, a closer look at the instances of China's alleged "theft" of Russian military technology in the 1990s made it clear that the Chinese State-Owned Enterprises (SOEs)

---

[22] J. Tianqin, W. Han, "In Depth: Investigation Casts Shadow on Rosneft's China Investor CEFC", *Caixin*, 1 March 2018.

had not brazenly stolen technology but simply taken advantage of loopholes in the Russian regulatory environment of the time. Moscow decided to exploit the remaining window of opportunity to sell its advanced military equipment to China. From the strategic point of view, the Kremlin determined that Beijing had no intention of invading the Russian Far East as had previously been suspected. It became obvious to the Russian leadership that China's strategic military interest was now focused on the East and South China Seas (tension in both areas became higher around the same time). Furthermore, the thorough risk assessment undertaken by Moscow in 2014 concluded that if Beijing did offer any aggression, the Russian military would have the nuclear and conventional capability to deter such threats. The Kremlin did remain wary, however, of selling China any weapons still under test and not yet issued to the Russian military itself (hypersonic weapons, the S-500 surface-to-air missile, etc.)[23].

In 2015 Moscow sold China the S-400, its most advanced anti-aircraft missile system (the next generation, S-500, is under test), and its latest jet fighter, the Su-35. Russian weapons are crucial to the Chinese military build-up in the East and South China Seas as well as in the Taiwan Strait, as tension with the US increases in those areas. Russia and China have also strengthened their military ties with a series of joint military exercises: naval exercises in the Mediterranean in 2015, in the South China Sea in 2016, and in the East China Sea and the Baltic in 2017. Between 2016 and 2018 they have held various land exercises which should be seen as a response to the expansion of US anti-missile defense systems in Europe and Asia, including deployments of the THAAD system in South Korea and the Aegis Ashore system in Japan[24].

---

[23] A. Gabuev, V. Kashin, *Vooruzhennaya druzhba: kak Rossija I Kitaj torgujut oruzhiem* (*Armed Friendship: How Russia and China Trade in Weaponry*), Carnegie Moscow Center, 2 November 2017.

[24] M. Swaine, "Chinese Views on South Korea's Deployment of THAAD", *China Leadership Monitor*, vol. 52, 2 February 2017, pp. 1-15.

Current Trends: Geopolitical Rapprochement

Intensified military exchanges between China and Russia in recent years have sparked discussions in the West about a potential military alliance between them[25], but deepening military cooperation does not amount to alliance-building. Despite their increased military exchanges and other forms of strategic cooperation, global Chinese and Russian interests are not always aligned, and any alliance would, therefore, be impractical for the two countries. Beijing does not want to be formally dragged into Moscow's quarrel with the West in addition to the growing strains in Sino-US relations. Moscow, on the other hand, is aware of the risks that an official alliance with Beijing would pose to its ties with India and Vietnam, important geopolitical and trade partners. Some senior officers in Russia's armed forces do argue, however, that the possibility of an alliance between China and Russia should not be dismissed out of hand if the American pressure against both countries continues to build.

All the same, the geopolitical rapprochement between Moscow and Beijing has continued since 2014. In 2015, Xi Jinping was the only great power leader to attend a military parade in Moscow to mark the 70th anniversary of USSR victory in World War II. All Western Heads of State ignored the event because of the ongoing confrontation over Crimea. After a headline-making bilateral summit in 2014, Xi's visit to a Russia ostracised by the entire West was a great geopolitical boost to the Kremlin; and Putin and Xi have met each other more than once a year since then. At these bilateral summits, the heads of government usually exchange the highest state honours and watch as Russian and Chinese state companies sign piles of agreements, many impressively ambitious but of little substantive content[26].

---

[25] G. Allison, "China and Russia: A Strategic Alliance in the Making", *The National Interest*, 14 December 2018.
[26] N. Ng, P. Stronski, *Cooperation and Competition: Russia and China in Central Asia,*

Moscow's decision that Beijing does not pose significant threats to it, at least in the short term, has reconfigured the relationship between the two countries on the world stage. This axis can be seen in many areas of Sino-Russian geopolitical engagement and is often misperceived in the West as alliance-building, but the official stance in China and Russia alike is wary of bold statements about an alliance; at times they pursue separate interests around the world, but never openly contradict each other[27].

Division of labour in Central Asia

In Central Asia, an area traditionally viewed by the Kremlin as its own backyard[28], China has been raising its profile since the early 2000s when Chinese state-owned enterprises started to actively invest in the region under Beijing's "Going Out" policy. Rich in resources, poor in infrastructure and hungry for capital, the countries of Central Asia became vitally important to China's energy security and offered diversification in the mid-2000s when oil and gas first flowed through pipelines from Kazakhstan and Turkmenistan. Their importance to Beijing grew further with the announcement of the Belt and Road Initiative in 2013 and the billions of dollars invested in their infrastructure.

China's expanding role in Central Asia is still regarded by many as a potential source of trouble between Moscow and Beijing, but that was not the conclusion drawn in the Kremlin's multidimensional risk assessment of China. The issue of Central Asia was handled by Igor Shuvalov, the First Deputy Prime Minister, known as a "fixer" for Vladimir Putin's inner circle. He argued convincingly that it was both natural and

---

the Russian Far East, and the Arctic, Carnegie Endowment for the International Peace, 28 February 2018.

[27] Y. Trofimov, "The New Beijing-Moscow Axis", *The Wall Street Journal*, 1 February 2019.

[28] J. Farchy, "China's Great Game: In Russia's Backyard", *Financial Times*, 14 October 2015.

inevitable for Chinese economic influence in Central Asia to grow. Moscow realised that it would have to compete with the Central Asian countries for resource deals and investment from China, besides facing the geopolitical confrontation with Europe. Russian leaders understood the folly of any attempt to challenge China's economic penetration of Central Asia, where Beijing had been gaining influence as a major trade and investment partner; instead, they decided to seek a division of labour in the region with Beijing: Russia would wield the gun and China the money, but on condition that it respected Russia-led multilateral mechanisms in the region such as the Eurasian Economic Union.

Never against each other: Crimea, South China Sea, and North Korea

In 2014-2016, Moscow and Beijing took turns at standing in the crossfire of each other's geopolitical slanging match with the West. The Russian annexation of Crimea was a hot potato for China, for Moscow's actions in Ukraine exemplified one of Beijing's greatest fears: Russian military support for nationalist separatism in Crimea inevitably reminded the Chinese leadership of potential similarities in their own country's traditionally "difficult" regions of Xinjiang and Tibet[29]. Trying not to criticise the Kremlin, Beijing called for Ukrainian territorial integrity but abstained from the UN resolution vote, citing its long-standing principle of non-interference.

Two years later the Kremlin faced a similar geopolitical quandary over China. In 2016 Moscow had to settle its position on the territorial dispute in the South China Sea. As the Philippines prosecuted a lawsuit against China in the international arbitral tribunal and the West's condemnation of China was unravelling, the Russian Foreign Ministry took a restrained stance, calling for a diplomatic solution of the dispute without

---

[29] A. Gabuev, *Friends With Benefits? Russian-Chinese Relations After the Ukraine Crisis*, Carnegie Moscow Center, 29 June 2016.

interference in the issue by third parties. Cautious about the effect which any concrete statement on the South China Sea issue might have on its relationship with Hanoi (one of the biggest buyers of Russian military equipment), Moscow did not openly side with Beijing on its territorial claims, but it also never formally opposed China's actions in the region[30].

The newly-established Kremlin-Zhongnanhai axis was tested again in 2017, when the North Korean crisis gained renewed momentum with hawkish rhetoric from the US President Donald Trump. While Beijing cooperatively joined in the negotiations as a major power along with the US, Moscow successfully played the "bad cop" role, watering down the programme of UN sanctions in response to Pyongyang's nuclear tests that would inevitably have led to the regime's collapse due to a complete ban on oil shipments[31].

Moscow and Beijing have disagreed, however, on certain geopolitical issues. The recent SCO expansion to include both India and Pakistan shows that China and Russia might have different agendas even within the multilateral organisations they themselves created. Moscow had been pushing since 2011 for the SCO to offer membership to its long-standing partner India, as a way of limiting China's influence within the organisation: Moscow argued that Russia, China, and India were already working together and that India's joining the SCO would only increase its scope. The expectation in the Kremlin was that the addition of another rising Asian giant would hold back China's prospects of dominating the SCO. Not surprisingly, China resisted the idea for a while, and in the end came up with a proposal to include Pakistan as well, a reliable partner highly dependent on China for loans and investment. The expansion of the SCO to include the historic rivals India and Pakistan not only diminished the organisation's ability to reach consensus on

---

[30] A. Tsvetov, "Did Russia Just Side With China on the South China Sea?", *The Diplomat*, 21 April 2016.

[31] A. Gabuev, "China and Russia's Dangerous Entente", *The Wall Street Journal*, 4 October 2017.

regional issues, but has also shed light on the disagreements and potential tensions that the geopolitical engagement between China and Russia might face in future.

Conclusion: Asymmetric Interdependence

Before the clash with the West threatened Moscow with complete geopolitical isolation, China was well down Russia's list of geopolitical priorities. For over twenty years after the end of the Cold War, the Kremlin's view of China was based on a combination of fear and arrogance; but when Moscow's attempts to become a full member of the Western community failed, leading to serious conflict in 2014, it had to look in the other direction. In pursuit of geopolitical rebalancing, Moscow had no choice but to pivot to the East. Once the Ukrainian crisis had begun the Russian government quickly revised its attitude to China, discarded its long-standing fears and gradually adapted to its new role as Beijing's junior partner.

Moscow's rapprochement with Beijing is driven by geopolitical calculation and a sense of urgency brought on by its confrontation with the West; but it came at the time when China had already become the world's leading economic, military, and geopolitical power. Meanwhile, Russian GDP is no greater than that of Guangdong province, and its defense spending just one third of China's[32]. Russia is learning to adapt to this asymmetric dependence on China in exchange for formal respect from Beijing. In turn, China is more than ready to nourish and cherish the Kremlin's great power ambitions, as long as it has Moscow's backing on certain geopolitical issues as it expands the scale and scope of its international engagement.

Since Donald Trump took office in the US, the behaviour of the new administration in Washington has been driving Russia even closer to China. Despite Trump's rhetoric about plans to improve cooperation with Russia, two years of his presidency

---

[32] "Defense Spending by Country", *Global Fire Power*.

have not only achieved nothing positive in their relationship but have actually brought cooperation between the countries to a new low. The US Congress has managed to pass a bill that practically sets sanctions against Russia in stone, and marks a new era in the relationship between Moscow and the West. In August 2017, when Donald Trump was obliged to sign new Russian sanctions into law, the Russian elite realised that those sanctions are the new reality of their relationship with Washington. The Kremlin has no illusions about the prospects of cooperation with the White House in the near future: Russian leaders still remember the Jackson-Vanik amendment of 1974 applying sanctions to the USSR for restricting Jewish emigration. The US Congress rescinded that amendment only in 2013, and it was quickly replaced with the Magnitskiy Act punishing the Russian officials involved in the death of Sergei Magnitsky, a tax accountant who revealed a US$230 million scheme corrupting the Russian tax authorities. Just as the Russian relationship with the US has reached its lowest point since the Cold War, Moscow's ties with the EU countries – who joined Washington in sanctioning Russia after the Ukrainian crisis in 2014 – have also significantly worsened[33].

Since Donald Trump's inauguration and the ongoing investigation into alleged Russian meddling with the 2016 US presidential elections, Moscow's prospects of improving relations with the West have become negligible. With little or nothing in the way of alternatives, Moscow has been forced to seek even broader cooperation with Beijing than it was willing to contemplate during the Ukraine crisis of 2014. China maintains the upper hand in its relationship with Russia, thanks to its economic clout and its worldwide geopolitical influence. After decades of being Beijing's "elder brother", Moscow now finds itself needing China more than China needs it. Beijing is happy to have Moscow back its major geopolitical initiatives, for it has

---

[33] K. Manson, C. Weaver, and M. Peel, "US presses Europe for tougher sanctions on Russia", *Financial Times*, 24 May 2018.

its own points of tension with the West: the trade war with the US, and growing general alarm about China's rise. Moscow and Beijing have developed a model of asymmetric interdependence that works well for both of them, at least in the short or medium term.

3. Russia and China: An Enhanced Security Cooperation

Alessandro Arduino

The geopolitical importance of Eurasia, defined here as the combined landmasses of Europe and Asia, has increased over the past decade. This development has the potential for a fundamental shift in international security cooperation, especially in light of the vacuum caused by the withdrawal of the United States from the international scene. Under his "America First" policy President Donald Trump has indeed taken a number of unilateral actions, withdrawing from the Trans-Pacific Partnership and more recently running down the military US presence in Afghanistan while sending out confusing signals about America's military commitment to Syria. The negative impact of the Trump administration's vacillation and retreat from America's international commitments has been compounded as the European Union has gradually retrenched its international reach along the Mediterranean littoral, partly because of the complex socioeconomic constraints resulting from the global market crash of 2008.

Meanwhile, the impact of China's economic influence and the effects of a resurgent Russia on the international scene have over the past few years encouraged a process of strategic integration between Beijing and Moscow. It has yet to be seen whether this inchoate bilateral integration can transform the current world order, as both China and Russia are playing a game of cooperation and competition that will involve significant points of friction in the years ahead. Even if this new model of bilateral international cooperation has not yet posed a significant challenge to the Western-dominated architecture of global governance, it has already started to provide alternatives to the unipolar model of American hegemony in both economic and security terms.

In economic terms, China's Belt and Road Initiative (BRI) is a game changer that has the potential to fill substantial gaps in the funding of infrastructure across more than 70 countries on three continents. The BRI is the signature foreign policy priority of Chinese President Xi Jinping, and its planned economic investment could total US$4 trillion, affecting more than two thirds of the world's population and more than one third of global economic output[1]. The financial support and connectivity provided by the Silk Road Economic Belt (SREB) have created positive externalities such as improved regional cooperation and trade, but the venture has also increased the possibility of criminal and political violence against Chinese outward investments and expatriate personnel. China's Eurasian moves have nudged Russia into revamping its own economic initiatives in the region, the Eurasian Economic Union and the Greater Eurasian Partnership[2].

In terms of security, the most tangible expression of the Eurasian cooperation model has been the Shanghai Cooperation Organisation (SCO). That organisation reflects Chinese and Russian security priorities for Eurasia, from improved military-to-military relations to interoperability in dealing with non-conventional threats. The recent expansion of the SCO has displayed a new model of international security

---

[1] A. Arduino, X. Gong, *Securing the Belt & Road Initiative. Risk Assessment, Private Security and Special Insurances along the new wave of Chinese Outbound Investments*, Palgrave, 2018.

[2] N. Rolland, "A China-Russia Condominium over Eurasia. China and Russia share similar views of what a future Eurasian order should look like", *Survival: Global Politics and Strategy*, February/March 2019, International Institute for Strategic Studies (IISS), January 2019.

cooperation, though one not intended – at least for the time being – to challenge the *status quo*. China is expanding its geopolitical footprint in Eurasia, but Russia remains a key player due to economic ties, the Eurasian Economic Union, the security role of the Collective Security Treaty Organization (CSTO), and Russia's normative, cultural and linguistic soft power[3]. Not only is China unable to contest Russia's status as a prominent player in security matters, but Beijing also shares common concerns with Moscow on security problems in Central and South Asia, including extremism, terrorism, illicit trade, gun-running and drug smuggling. Given the ISAF (International Security Assistance Force) coalition's planned withdrawal of forces from Afghanistan and the reduction of US security cover in Iraq and Syria, China and Russia have intensified their dialogue on security cooperation. Despite its decades-old foreign policy of non-interference, China is being drawn further and further into the region's security issues by its involvement in the SREB and in particular by the China-Pakistan Economic Corridor (CPEC). Although the main link in relations between China and other BRI participants has been the supply of natural resources, China's unparalleled expansion into foreign infrastructure projects has already influenced bilateral and multilateral relationships[4].

In this chapter, I examine four aspects of Eurasia's growing importance. First, I discuss the full spectrum of security risks in Eurasia associated with the land segment of China's BRI, the SREB and the flagship project, the CPEC. Second, I consider how the multilateral SCO might be used to mitigate those risks. Thirdly, I look at the interaction between China and Russia, including both cooperation and confrontation in the context of providing security for the BRI; and finally, I explore the role of private security companies (PSCs) and the privatisation of the state's monopoly of force. The chapter draws on my previous

---

[3] A. Arduino, X. Gong (2018).
[4] F.-P. van der Putten, J. Seaman, M. Huotari, A. Ekman, and M. Otero-Iglesias, *Europe and China's New Silk Roads*, ETNC Report, December 2016.

publications including *Securing the Belt and Road Initiative* and *China's Private Army*, as well as new research work assessing the security implications of the SREB for China's domestic and foreign policy and for Russia.

The Belt and Road Initiative: Security Requirements

The Belt and Road Initiative, which is the signature foreign policy of Chinese President Xi Jinping, was recently enshrined in the constitution of the Chinese Communist Party[5]. The BRI has two main arms: the SREB, a land route starting in western China that goes through Central Asia and on to the Middle East with its terminus in the European Union; and the XXI century Maritime Silk Road, a series of maritime routes connecting Southeast Asia with the Middle East and South Africa; this also reaches as far as the EU. While China and Russia play a prominent role in Eurasia, Turkey, India, Pakistan and Iran are intensifying their regional influence through historical, cultural and linguistic ties. The BRI, which was formally announced by President Xi in 2013, is now in its sixth year. By the first half of 2018 total Chinese investment in BRI development projects in more than 70 countries surpassed US$300 billion[6]. Natural resource exploitation has been the initial priority, to be followed by investments in logistics and energy infrastructure. The BRI is promoted as an economic opportunity. In particular, the SREB aims to link Eurasia via a network of railways, roads, pipelines, ICT and power grids. Central Asia is at the heart of the overland route, which starts from the Chinese Uyghur Autonomous Province of Xinjiang and crosses Mongolia, Kazakhstan, Kyrgyzstan, Tajikistan, Uzbekistan,

---

[5] Resolution approved by the 19th CPC National Congress "'Belt and Road' incorporated into CPC Constitution", *Xinhua*, 24 October 2017.

[6] J. Shuiyu, "Belt and Road Initiative Exceeds Initial Expectations", Chinadaily.com.cn, 11 April 2017.

and Turkmenistan. The SREB links China with the European Union, and with the Arabian Peninsula via the CPEC. The BRI also showcases China's preferred strategic and diplomatic tool, which is economic power[7]. China's use of economic means to promote its security interests and to shape global security institutions and norms is generating anxiety in various circles[8].

The political and criminal violence affecting the BRI, especially the killing of Chinese citizens from Mali to Pakistan along BRI corridors, is forcing Beijing's strategic planners to contemplate changes to their decades-old principle of non-interference. A crucial part of this evolutionary process relates to Beijing's ability to quickly improve its risk prevention and mitigation capabilities along the sea lines of communication and the Eurasian land belt[9].

The SREB land route involves a wide array of non-traditional security issues. Some areas in Central Asia are exposed to ethnic and religious tensions, while in Pakistan and Afghanistan a broader spectrum of political and criminal violence is already affecting the development of the CPEC[10]. Pakistan and China have made bilateral agreements to increase the already remarkable budget of US$62 billion devoted to the economic corridor[11]. The aim of the CPEC is to connect China's northwest Xinjiang Uyghur Autonomous Region with the deep-water port at Gwadar in south-western Pakistan by means of a network of roads, railways and energy projects; but the newly elected

---

[7] D. Bräutigam, T. Xiaoyang, "Economic statecraft in China's new overseas special economic zones: soft power, business or resource security?", *International Affairs*, Oxford University Press, vol. 88, no. 4, July 2012, pp. 799-816.
[8] M. Huotari, J. Gaspers, T. Eder, H. Legarda, and S. Mokry, *China's Emergence as a Global Security Actor. Strategies for Europe*, MERICS, Papers on China, , July 2017.
[9] Shanghai shihui kexue yuan, Yidaiyilu zhiku baogao di 1/2 qi, (Shanghai Academy of Social Sciences, *2018 Belt and Road Think Tank Report*, vol. 1/2), 28 February 2018.
[10] A. Arduino, *China-Pakistan Economic Corridor: Security and Inclusive Development Needed*, University of Nottingham's Asia Research Institute, 18 July 2017.
[11] S. Zheng, "Is China's US$62 billion investment plan fuelling resentment in Pakistan?", *South China Morning Post*, 3 July 2018.

Pakistani Prime Minister Imran Khan is seeking to renegotiate the financial terms with Beijing, and worsening security issues are slowing the pace of investment on the Chinese side. Beijing is well aware that in order to achieve President Xi's vision for a "big family of harmonious co-existence"[12] a wide range of security cooperation mechanisms need to be established and activated. Because of the huge area covered by BRI corridors, a growing number of Chinese companies are attempting to work in environments made extremely dangerous by armed conflicts, social tensions and organised crime, as well as weak and predatory governments. These conditions involve a wide array of risks that expose Chinese assets and Chinese citizens to considerable danger; so risk assessment and risk mitigation are key variables in the equation for many BRI projects.

As previously mentioned, separatist and extremist threats affect Pakistan's long-term development, while its porous borders with Afghanistan can only increase the probability of conflict. Also, from a geopolitical standpoint, India's anxiety and distrust over what it feels are hidden agendas agreed in Beijing and Islamabad are affecting the BRI's win-win narrative. At the same time, both India and Pakistan have recently joined the SCO as full members, and that multilateral organisation might promote a diplomatic solution to the two countries decades-old security problems – or it might get entangled in the process. Similarly, Saudi distrust over the role of the BRI in connecting Iran and Pakistan is already increasing anxiety over the new energy trade routes that will link the Persian Gulf directly to China. According to James Dorsey[13], India sees the greater capacity at Gwadar as a threat to Mumbai's support in developing the Iranian port of Chambhar.

Conversely, from the Saudi point of view, the efficiency of the new trade route will feed Iran's growing ambitions as a regional power. Sino-Pakistani cooperation as part of several

---

[12] Xi Jinping, keynote speech at the opening ceremony of the Belt and Road Forum (BRF) for International Cooperation in Beijing, 14 May 2017, http://www.xinhuanet.com//english/2017-05/14/c_136282982.htm.

[13] J. Dorsey, *China and the Middle East: Venturing into the Maelstrom*, Palgrave, 2018.

aspects of the BRI is not based on shared cultural or ideological values, but rather upon pragmatic economic needs and security constraints[14]. On a much larger scale, the same combination of security constraints and economic imperatives gives rise to compelling common interests between China and Russia. In this sense, the SCO is an expression of the evolving Eurasian geopolitical and security landscape.

The Shanghai Cooperation Organisation: Paving the Road for a New Eurasian Order?

The demise of the Soviet Union and the creation of the five Central Asian states Kazakhstan, Kyrgyzstan Uzbekistan, Tajikistan and Turkmenistan have caused tensions and unresolved disputes ranging from border delineation to water control. In 1996, the Shanghai Five group was established to solve the border disputes diplomatically and establish confidence-building measures to defuse possible military confrontation. The Shanghai Five successfully arranged armed force reductions in the border areas and then proceeded to work towards establishing further security and peace-building mechanisms. With the inclusion of Uzbekistan in 2001 the Shanghai Five group evolved into the multilateral Shanghai Cooperation Organization[15]. The SCO is a permanent intergovernmental organisation whose creation was announced on 15 June 2001 in Shanghai (China) by the Republic of Kazakhstan, the People's Republic of China, the Kyrgyz Republic, the Russian Federation, the Republic of Tajikistan, and the Republic of Uzbekistan. The SCO Charter was signed during the St Petersburg meeting of SCO Heads of State in June 2002 and came into force on 19 September 2003[16].

---

[14] A. Arduino (2017).
[15] Shanghai Cooperation Organization, *Declaration on the Establishment of the Shanghai Cooperation Organization*, Shanghai, 2001.
[16] *Ibid.*

Despite its name, the organisation's secretariat is based in Beijing; its general assembly is hosted by member states in turn for a year each. Vladimir Norov, former Minister of Foreign Affairs of the Republic of Uzbekistan, has been Secretary General since the beginning of 2019[17]. Beginning as a very specific cooperation mechanism set up to solve immediate security concerns following the demise of the Soviet Union, the organisation has evolved into a multilateral security organisation based on three pillars: security and regional governance, economic development, and the promotion of regional culture. In 17 years of continuous evolution, the SCO has grown from a Central Asian body to a broader regional cooperative organisation whose size, scope, and significance have now grown further with the recent inclusion of India and Pakistan. This latest expansion is a showcase for a new model of international relations, even if some critics point to its need to develop new mechanisms if it is to reach a broader consensus and overcome the "symbiotic distrust" between China and Russia[18], and others hint that enlargement will dilute the organisation's effectiveness[19].

In addition to the renewed interest in sustainable economic development and people-to-people cooperation, the SCO's security role in countering the "three evils" of terrorism, separatism, and extremism is at the core of the organisation's mission. According to the China Institute for International Studies, the SCO was the first institution of its kind formed to repress these three evils, and over the years it has built up a well-established legal system for security cooperation[20]. The

---

[17] "Vladimir Norov takes office as SCO Secretary General", UzDaily.com, 2 January 2019.
[18] A. Arduino, "China's Energy Interests in Central Asia and Russia: Symbiotic distrust and striking a balance between cooperation and confrontation", in Fengshi Wu, Hongzhou Zhang (eds.), *China's Global Quest for Resources Energy, Food and Water*, London-New York, Routledge, 2017.
[19] W. Piekos, E.C. Economy, *The Risks and Rewards of SCO Expansion*, Council on Foreign Relations (CFR), 7 July 2015.
[20] Z. Mingwen, *Shanghai Cooperation Organization: A New Stage, New Challenges, and

fight against terrorism is organised around RATS, the Regional Anti-Terrorism Structure, and its database sharing intelligence and best practice. The organisation also deals with drug trafficking, cross-border crime, and more recently the safeguarding of oil and gas pipelines. The practical aspects of security cooperation have taken the form of bilateral and multilateral security drills and war games such as "Coalition", "Coordination", and "Peace Mission", and of regular joint military anti-terrorism exercises for law enforcement authorities, including "East-2014", "Norak Anti-terror", "Solidarity" and "Tianshan". Unlike the CSTO, the SCO is not a military alliance with pooled armed forces; most of its war games concentrate on counterinsurgency drills rather than on conventional warfare. According to de Haas[21] the leading role of Russia in the CSTO, and of both Russia and China in the SCO, is reflected in these military exercises as well.

The SCO may be regarded as the two countries' preferred forum for their engagement not only in Central Asia but more broadly, covering Eurasian security aspects which now include South Asia and Syria. Nevertheless, China's priorities and the fluidity of relations between Beijing and Moscow play a key role in shaping cooperation within that organisation.

Throughout 2018 the threat created by foreign fighters returning home from the Middle East, especially from Syria, has increased. From the SCO standpoint, these returning veterans present a clear and present danger. Shared security concerns, especially over Syria and Afghanistan, were highlighted at the organisation's latest summit (the 18th Meeting of the Council of Heads of Member States in Qingdao, China), and the SCO issued several warnings about this "terrorist spillover"[22]. From

---

A New Journey, China Institute for International Studies (CIIS), August 2018.

[21] M. de Haas, "War Games of the Shanghai Cooperation Organization and the Collective Security Treaty Organization: Drills on the Move!", *The Journal of Slavic Military Studies*, vol. 29, no. 3, 2016, pp. 378-406, DOI: 10.1080/13518046.2016.1200383

[22] "R. Alimov: Qingdao summit to show SCO's growing role in global affairs",

Beijing's perspective, if the efforts to stabilise Syria are not managed correctly, the resulting insecurity will not only have a negative influence on the BRI but will also undermine China's policies in the Xinjiang Uyghur Autonomous Region.

There are no reliable estimates of the number of Uyghur fighters who have joined the Turkistan Islamic Party (TIP) or the self-proclaimed Islamic State fighting in Syria: estimates range from hundreds to thousands. During 2017 and 2018 some analysts cautiously suggested that Beijing might be getting dragged into the Middle East quagmire by deploying the People's Liberation Army (PLA) to combat the terrorist menace in Syria. Chinese military deployment against the TIP remains a very remote possibility in 2019: Beijing's focus is rather on economic reconstruction[23]. Nevertheless, a greater Chinese economic footprint in Syria might well provoke local terrorist attacks on Chinese companies as a convenient proxy for President Assad's regime[24]. Furthermore, the loss of land-based support for the IS in Iraq and Syria exacerbates two dangers: foreign fighters returning home, and the spread of terrorist ideology leading to a proliferation of extremist networks in Eurasia. Russia is already involved in Syrian hostilities, but China and other SCO member countries are increasingly having to consider how to contain the terrorist spillover before it becomes an acute problem.

During the Qingdao summit, Xi Jinping emphasised the imperative need for cooperation and security if the momentum of Eurasia's economic growth was to be sustained[25]. Several security and containment issues were discussed during the meeting, including the Russian involvement in Syria and the

---

Tass Russian New Agency, 5 June 2018.

[23] A. Arduino, "Syrian peace dividends for China in 2019. The competition for business opportunities in Syria will insert China into competitive cooperation with Russian, Iranian and Lebanese firms", *The Arab Weekly*, 5 January 2019.

[24] M. Duchâtel, "China's foreign fighters problem", *War on the Rocks*, 25 January 2019.

[25] Xi Jinping, "Carrying Forward the Shanghai Spirit to Build a Community with a Shared Future Remarks", *Xinhua*, June 2018.

Chinese efforts from 2016 onwards to resolve the conflict[26]. In this regard, the Wakhan corridor military base in Afghanistan and the provision of military hardware for the border forces of Tajikistan and Kyrgyzstan show a gradual shift in the Chinese attitude to military deployment abroad; and a broader Chinese diplomatic engagement with the Assad regime could be seen as Beijing's next step towards a more proactive policy. The evolution of Beijing's involvement in Syria and its cooperation with the Russian security umbrella to protect Chinese investments will shape the future of the SCO's counterterrorism efforts. Beijing is aware that its ambitious Belt and Road Initiative is fundamentally dependent on the political stability and security of the host countries.

The Impact of Terrorism on the BRI

As the Chinese economic footprint becomes larger and more diverse, so do the associated risks – one of which is terrorism. According to the 2018 Global Terrorism Index, 25,673 deaths were caused by terrorism in 2016, 13% fewer than in 2015. This is the second consecutive year that the number of deaths from terrorism has fallen[27]. The five countries with the highest recorded death toll from terrorism are still Afghanistan, Nigeria, Syria, Iraq and Pakistan, together accounting for three quarters of all such deaths. All five are countries where China has important investments; Afghanistan and Pakistan are directly linked with the Eurasian security nexus, and Syria and Iraq are generating dangerous ripples for the SREB: the collapse in land-based support for the self-proclaimed Islamic State in Iraq and Syria, in particular, poses a danger as foreign fighters return to their countries of origin.

---

[26] M. Chaziza, *China's Approach to Mediation in the Middle East: Between Conflict Resolution and Conflict Management*, Middle East Institute, 8 May 2018.
[27] Institute for Economics & Peace, *Global Terrorism Index 2018: Measuring the impact of terrorism*, Sydney, November 2018, http://visionofhumanity.org/reports

In conjunction with the long-term impact on geopolitical relations, Chinese investments face other local challenges. For instance, they have repeatedly come under the spotlight as a result of a perceived negative environmental and social impact on local communities. Security is also a concern: an important part of Chinese investment in infrastructure and energy is concentrated in developing countries, weak states, and areas with ethnic tensions and militant groups of various kinds. This means that Chinese workers and infrastructure are targeted by insurgents, rebels, and militants with motivations ranging from the political to the financial[28]. From Central Asia to the MENA region, the BRI's non-conventional security hazards include extremism and terrorism: Islamic State, al-Qaeda and the Turkistan Islamic Party, to name just a few. The TIP currently operates from Idlib in Syria, independently but in close cooperation with Hayat Tahir al Sham (HTS), or more broadly alongside various armed groups in Syria closer to Al Qaeda than to IS. There are also numerous off-shoots incorporating non-Uyghur ethnic fighters alongside Uyghurs, such as Katibat al Tawhid wal Jihad (KTJ). In the past, China has managed to avoid getting entangled in international conflicts and disputes; but the global reach of the BRI is now forcing it to become a security provider, albeit unwillingly. Examples of China's expanding security footprint include the first overseas PLA base in Djibouti, joint patrols along the Mekong River by the Chinese People's Armed Police (PAP), and a peacekeeping mission in Africa under the aegis of the United Nations. The CPEC, in one of the most troubled areas of Chinese investment, has already seen several acts of violence: since February 2018 there has been an increase in threats against Chinese nationals in Pakistan, and attacks on them have included the assassination of the Regional General Manager of COSCO Shipping Lines in the port city of Karachi. A bus carrying Chinese mine workers was targeted by a suicide bomber in Baluchistan province the following August,

---

[28] A. Arduino, X. Gong (2018).

and Islamic State had earlier beheaded two Chinese teachers in the Quetta area.

The first acknowledged terrorist attack on a Chinese diplomatic mission occurred in Central Asia in the capital of the Kyrgyz Republic, where on 30 August 2016 a car rammed through the gates of the Chinese Embassy in Bishkek, allegedly driven by an Uyghur with a forged Tajik passport who died after detonating an explosive device. A year later a Kyrgyz court sentenced three Kyrgyz citizens to jail for providing financial and logistical support for the attack and being supporters of the TIP. The second took place in the Balochi port city of Karachi on November 23 2018, when the Chinese Consulate General was targeted by terrorists armed with automatic rifles and hand grenades. Two Pakistani policemen, several bystanders and three terrorists died[29].

The external risk to the BRI's development is compounded by domestic dangers originating in the Xinjiang Uyghur Autonomous Region, which – among other things – is the starting point of the New Silk Road. Xinjiang is the natural geographic link between China, on the one hand, and South and Central Asia, on the other hand. Therefore, the province is essential to the sustainable development of the BRI, but it is also vulnerable to Islamic extremists and independence movements. The situation in Xinjiang has recently provoked an international uproar concerning the treatment of ethnic Uyghurs, and the Chinese government's account of the Xinjiang situation has come under scrutiny by the international media as a result. At the same time, China faces a threat posed by the return of battle-hardened Uyghurs who fought alongside the TIP or Islamic State (IS)[30].

---

[29] "China confirms, condemns attack on consulate in Pakistan's Karachi", *Xinhua*, 23 November 2018.
[30] A. Arduino, N. Soliev, "Malhama Tactical Threatens to Put China in its Crosshairs", *Terrorism Monitor*, vol. 15, no. 22, The Jamestown Foundation, 27 November 2017.

Next door, the China-Pakistan Economic Corridor is at great risk from the instability of the political environment in Pakistan and Afghanistan where terrorist attacks have become frequent. The US-led war on terror in Afghanistan resulted in the capture of several dozen Uyghur militants in 2001 and 2002 and revealed their involvement with the Islamic Movement of Uzbekistan (IMU) as well as their affiliation with the Taliban. Jacob Zenn's research on the origins of the TIP, from the IMU to today's involvement in the Syrian conflict[31], suggests that its first members were among those Uyghurs who fled Xinjiang in the 1990s to avoid a police crackdown on separatist movements and found sanctuary and military training in Afghanistan, then under the Taliban. Their more recent involvement in the Syrian civil war led some TIP members to opt for jihad under the black banner of the "caliphate" rather than with the Taliban.

Following many acts of violence in Xinjiang during 2008 and 2009 there have been very few attacks by Uyghurs in China during the last ten years; but according to Nodirbek Soliev[32] that should not be seen as indicating that the volatile province will enjoy lasting peace and stability in the long run. The government campaign to "re-educate" the province's Muslim minorities could still be fuelling long-term resentments.

As for Russia, President Vladimir Putin has been promoting the idea of a global Western anti-terrorism coalition including the European Union and the United States since 2000[33]. That year, Moscow supported UN sanctions against the Taliban regime; and well before the September 11 attacks, Russia had been warning of terrorist training camps in Afghanistan and

---

[31] J. Zenn, "The Turkistan Islamic Party in Double-Exile: Geographic and Organizational Divisions in Uighur Jihadism", *Terrorism Monitor*, vol. 16, no. 17, The Jamestown Foundation, 7 September 2018.
[32] N. Soliev, *Uyghur Violence and Jihadism in China and Beyond*, RSIS Counter Terrorist Trends and Analyses, January 2019.
[33] F. Hill, *Putin and Bush in Common Cause? Russia's View of the Terrorist Threat After September 11*, Brookings, 1 June 2002.

well-financed terrorist networks[34]. Though Washington and Moscow initially issued joint communiqués calling for cooperation against the terrorist menace, there were differences in their perceptions of the threat and their security responses; as a result, there were few occasions for cooperation, and the steady deterioration of US-Russian relations affected their common response to terrorism as to much else.

China looks like a more suitable partner for Russia's anti-terrorism activities. Firstly, the two countries' views on the nature and implications of the terrorist threat are similar: while the US perceives terrorism as an external threat from various states and non-state actors, Russia and China see terrorism, separatism, and religious extremism as primarily a domestic menace that generates social disorder and compromises national unity. Second, the two countries can count on a shared institution to help them combat terrorism: the SCO provides a means of upgrading Chinese counter-terrorism capabilities with the benefit of Russian experience, and the latest war games are designed to enhance interoperability in confronting non-conventional forces.

In this respect, Russia's recent engagement in Syria and the increasing role outside Russia of its Private Military Security Companies (PMSCs) offer China an alternative to Western-led counter-terrorism efforts and the Western-led privatisation of the monopoly of force. Since 2018 the Russian presence in the Middle East has reached levels not seen since the Soviet era in the 1960s and 1970s. Syria is one of Russia's closest Middle Eastern allies, but in 2019 China's economic diplomacy is putting the BRI at the heart of Assad's reconstruction process[35], giving Beijing and Moscow another arena for both security cooperation and economic confrontation.

---

[34] *Ibid.*
[35] D. Hemenway, *Chinese Strategic Engagement with Assad's Syria*, The Atlantic Council, 21 September 2018.

The Dragon and the Bear: Security Competition and Cooperation

While China's economic relationships are developing rapidly in Eurasia, and especially in Central and South Asia, Beijing's primary security concern in the region is still the peaceful development of its Xinjiang Uyghur Autonomous Region, which shares 2,800km of borders with Kazakhstan, Kyrgyzstan and Tajikistan. The region is also a prime example of the thin line between cooperation and competition on the part of China and Russia. Since the demise of the Soviet Union, Central Asia's energy, natural resources and geo-strategic interests have progressively been drawn into China's sphere of economic influence. The widespread notion that China is in charge of Central Asia's economic development while Russia has exclusive control of security is an oversimplification: the flow of outward financial investment across China's borders is accompanied by transfers of military hardware to its neighbours as well. The most recent SCO war games showcased the latest Chinese military products, available with financial support from Chinese government-led investment banks[36]. At the same time, Beijing's infrastructure investments in Kazakhstan, Kyrgyzstan, Tajikistan, Turkmenistan, and Uzbekistan are already promoting economic integration and regional security. Though the expanding role of the BRI has caused international anxiety over increasing Chinese political influence, it is bilateral trade with Russia and the economic partnership of its Eurasian Economic Union (EAEU) which are still predominant in several Central Asian countries[37].

The Ukraine crisis led to a revival of the Sino-Russian Strategic Partnership[38]. Russia's eastward shift in foreign policy since 2014 is well illustrated by a US$400 billion gas supply

---

[36] S. Ramani, "China's Expanding Security Cooperation With Tajikistan", *The Diplomat*, 16 July 2016.
[37] Stratford Worldview, *Central Asia's Economic Evolution from Russia To China*, April 2018.
[38] See chapter 2 in this volume.

agreement with China. Since then, several summit meetings between Chinese president Xi Jinping and his Russian counterpart Vladimir Putin have produced agreements for greatly expanded bilateral trade. Although oil and gas supplies are the main topics, military hardware transfers involving highly sophisticated weapon platforms are also on the rise. The Russian-led EAEU has softened its tone against China's New Silk Road. While the EAEU's ability to moderate Beijing's economic influence in Central Asia is relatively weak, Moscow's is still clearly willing to maintain a firm grip on regional security. The current Chinese-Russian alignment has already spread doubts and anxieties about a possible security axis designed to destabilise the current geopolitical balance. Eyebrows have already been raised in NATO at the 2018 Vostok training war games where 300,000 Russian soldiers manoeuvred alongside more than 3,000 Chinese. While some portray Sino-Russian cooperation, especially in the energy sector, as no more than mercantilist pragmatism devoid of any geopolitical calculation, others have concluded that both China and Russia have taken up a clear anti-American posture. Wang Xiaoguang characterises Russia's energy diplomacy policies and China's BRI as mostly "mercantile" in handling their respective domestic challenges over the short and medium terms without building political leadership[39]. Michael Case[40] portrays the common interests displayed by Beijing and Moscow as an increasing willingness to challenge the US.

While China's economic growth is slowing due to trade frictions with the US, Western economies have suffered a record rise in unemployment and high government deficits. Similarly, the Russian economy continues to face structural strains, a lack of infrastructure investment and over-reliance on energy exports. Despite the looming trade war with the US, the "market

---

[39] W. Xiaoguang, "Leadership-building dilemmas in emerging powers' economic diplomacy: Russia's energy diplomacy and China's OBOR", *Asia Europe Journal*, February 2019.

[40] M.S. Case et al., *Russia - China Relations. Assessing Common Ground and Strategic Fault Lines*, NBR Special Report 66, July 2017.

economy with Chinese characteristics" continues to assert its influence in Eurasia[41]. The latest expression of approval for China's state-led capitalism came from Russia's endorsement of the BRI, though some critics see this as due to a lack of alternatives. As a result, the Eurasian Economic Union has softened the tone of its competition with the Chinese economic order led by the BRI. In this regard, Russia's policy pivot toward Eurasia is also intended to shield Moscow against the Western sanctions imposed over Russia's annexation of the Crimea peninsula and the crisis in eastern Ukraine. The 2018 Eastern Economic Forum in Vladivostok showcased a revived comprehensive strategic partnership between Russia and China.

As the BRI expands along the New Silk Road corridors, the Chinese State-Owned Enterprises (SOEs) that are spearheading the initiative's state-led investments are exposed to a wide array of risks that are currently in dire need of a solution. The Chinese investment risk matrix includes not only financial risks and imperilled returns on investment (ROI): also, the various countries hosting Chinese investments cannot fully guarantee the safety of Chinese workers, as shown by the terrorist incidents mentioned earlier. Beijing has already realised that promoting economic prosperity is only one part of the solution and indeed, in some specific cases, part of the problem. Beijing is, therefore, trying to defuse and mitigate possible crises by enhancing its military capacity to reach troubled flashpoints, intensifying the transfer of military hardware, and promoting the development of a professional private security industry. Moscow is following the same pattern, but with different outcomes. The Russian army's level of professionalisation is already established, and the recent reforms enacted by President Vladimir Putin aim at creating a leaner and more efficient fighting force. Russia, too, is experiencing an increase in the popularity of employment in PMSCs that offer active military support[42]. The services provided by the Chinese

---

[41] A. Arduino, X. Gong (2018).
[42] C.R. Spea, "Russia's Military and Security Privatization, Nontraditional War", *Parameters*, vol. 48, no. 2, Summer 2018.

PSCs, though, concern protecting infrastructure and personnel; compared with their customarily passive stance, Russian PMSCs are closer to hybrid warfare[43].

From a Chinese standpoint, the purpose of the Chinese PSCs is to protect the SOEs and private Chinese SMEs in dangerous places. The security challenges of the BRI could be mitigated in a number of ways. The financial vehicles that support the macro projects are of primary importance, but the human security they require should not be overlooked. China's foreign currency reserves cannot alone guarantee Beijing's capacity or willingness to sustain the BRI at its initial pace. Like financial risks, security requirements also need to be viewed from a long-term perspective.

The privatisation of the security function: the role of Private Security Companies

Chinese companies openly acknowledge that there are numerous risks associated with their investments in emerging economies. In several cases, from the Chinese SOEs to the private sector SMEs, there is still a need to deploy a wide array of security tools including risk assessment, risk mitigation and crisis management; but Chinese firms are still reluctant to provide a realistic security budget, apart from those SOEs (mainly natural resources, ICT and logistics infrastructure companies) that have themselves experienced staff security crises[44]. The unprecedented scale of BRI infrastructure projects has resulted in a significant number of Chinese personnel operating in various remote areas for months or even years.

Large-scale infrastructure projects face an evolving range of security challenges. Even if an area is perceived as low-risk, the dynamic created by the sudden arrival of a large foreign workforce can create a challenging security environment. In Ethiopia, the construction of the electric railway connecting Addis Ababa

---

[43] A. Arduino, *China Private Army. Protecting the New Silk Road*, Palgrave, 2017.
[44] *Ibid.*

with Djibouti and the planned gas pipeline across the Ogaden basin are vulnerable to resistance from armed nomadic communities. Kidnapping for ransom (K&R) by terrorists or criminal gangs may still happen. Along the three corridors of the CPEC there is still the possibility of local acts of violence and especially K&R, despite the 15,000 soldiers deployed by Islamabad to protect local and foreign workers[45]. K&R risk is high in Central and Southern Africa, too, as well as other areas such as the MENA region, South America and even in ASEAN countries. According to Control Risks[46], "certain parts of the BRI six proposed corridors present a risk of K&R that should feature in an organisation's security strategy". The K&R threat matrix involves a wide range of actors, including pirates along the Somali coast and in the Strait of Malacca, international organised crime, and extreme Islamists operating in parts of Central and South Asia, the Middle East and East Africa.

A dangerous and volatile mix of high unemployment, widespread poverty and the inability of weak states to enforce the rule of law creates opportunities for local acts of violence against foreign-funded projects. Foreign workers along the BRI, especially Chinese management teams from the SOEs in charge of the infrastructure project, are a favourite target and offer the greatest rewards in money or publicity. The high cost of professional security from PSCs probably leads some companies, especially SMEs, to neglect proactive risk mitigation and address the problem only after a disaster has occurred.

Using PSCs to guard the BRI requires a wide range of security services, deployed along both land and sea corridors (Road and Belt, respectively). Terrorist threats are a present danger, but more often than not it is criminal violence or local business disputes that pose the greatest danger to Chinese investments,

---

[45] J.M. Dorsey, "Chinese engineer's disappearance takes on geopolitical significance", *Huffpost*, 17 January 2018.

[46] S. Boe, T. Campos, "Kidnapping risk along the Belt and Road Initiative", Control Risks official website, September 2017.

though such hazards get less publicity[47]. Even in areas formerly free of terrorist threats or other high security risks the sudden presence of hundreds of male Chinese workers and the amount of Chinese cash flowing into the local economy often create disparities and friction within the community. Male Chinese workers can create imbalances in areas where religious practices require the separation of men and women. Chinese workers' higher spending capacity can complicate matters further by generating resentment in remote villages with limited access to medicine and food[48]. Many project assessments are still flawed by insufficient oversight, insufficiently funded assessment of political risks and poor awareness of the danger of criminal violence. While the SOEs in the energy and ICT sectors are quite adept at assessing and managing their personnel's security, the Chinese public and private companies that are becoming engaged for the first time in high-risk areas are still reluctant to invest in costly but necessary security measures; meanwhile there have been several cases of SOEs using Chinese SME subcontractors well aware of the risks but prevented by their low-profit margins from investing in professional security. As SOEs expand operations along the BRI, the evolution of their security requirements has profound implications at the geopolitical level, obliging Beijing to take further steps to provide diplomatic and security support to Chinese nationals abroad. It has also promoted cooperation with the international private security industry in the form of Western multinationals, Russian PMSCs and local security firms.

Chinese and Russian attitudes to Private Security Companies

The need to secure Chinese investments along the BRI has initiated a race among Chinese and international PSCs for the most lucrative contracts to protect high-value individuals, workers,

---

[47] A. Arduino (2017).
[48] *Ibid.*

and infrastructure all along the New Silk Road. The Chinese market for armed protection is still in its infancy, and Beijing is scrambling to find a proper legal framework that does not compromise its decades-old foreign policy principle of non-interference. At the same time, China's own PSCs with experience within China, Western companies with a long history of supporting US-led stabilisation efforts in Iraq and Afghanistan, and above all the new Russian PMSCs that have begun to offer[49] their services outside the Russian Federation are all actively looking for a slice of the BRI security pie. There are said to be 2,500 security contractors in Syria alone[50].

During the Iraqi and Afghanistan conflicts the role of PSCs mostly involved support to regular armies; but the security aspect of the BRI is unique in its wide geographical scope and the range of different political, religious and economic requirements that all have to be addressed by means of tailored security solutions: hence the new term "Private Military Security Company".

China lacks any meaningful long-term experience in employing security contractors abroad similar to that which Western companies accumulated by trial and error in the Iraqi and Afghani conflicts over the past two decades. It has accordingly imported various models from abroad, including the "Blackwater model" and more recently the Russian approach to PSCs. One PMSC (led by Mr Eric Prince, the founder of the US firm Blackwater) is the Frontier Service Group (FSG), a Hong Kong-based security, logistics and insurance company that works for its main shareholder, the Chinese state investment group CITIC[51].

Russia's recent use of PMSCs in Syria shows the need for a more complex classification of these PSCs. One criterion is the demand for proxy warfare: unlike the Soviet Union, Russia

---

[49] *Ibid.*
[50] "Syria war: Who are Russia's shadowy Wagner mercenaries?", *BBC News*, 23 February 2018.
[51] http://www.fsgroup.com/en/aboutfsg.html

has been unable to use satellite states to provide proxy forces in projecting power abroad for its political and economic purposes. The hybrid conflict in Ukraine is a good example of the role of "volunteers" and PMSCs. According to Denis Korotkov's[52] investigative reports on contemporary Russian contractors, the Russian intervention in Syria has featured heavily-armed contractors taking part in regime offensives.

Russian privatisation of the monopoly of force involves not only guarding infrastructure and personnel but also taking part in military action, in Syria for instance; it, therefore, has greater strategic geopolitical implications than that of China.

As the Chinese see it, the current role of local PSCs is to fill security gaps left uncovered by the inadequate rule of law in weak host countries or open to danger from terrorism or separatism. Chinese PSCs have not yet developed into a fully professional complement to the People's Liberation Army (PLA), but as Beijing is unwilling to deploy armed forces abroad the growth of PSCs with Chinese characteristics is highly probable. At present, their quantity is not matched by their quality, as most of these companies provide nothing more than unarmed security guards; but there is a steady evolution towards a professional security force capable of operating in the most dangerous areas.

A few Chinese PSCs have shown increasing capability for operations abroad, and the number of local Chinese PSCs is growing, thanks to their connection with various Chinese subcontractors on BRI projects in high-risk areas which have not made proper risk assessments. However, although domestic Chinese PSCs collectively employ hundreds or even thousands of unarmed security personnel their international presence is still limited compared to the Western counterparts[53]. Some Chinese PSCs prefer to form joint ventures (JVs) with local or international security operators, farming out the armed security

---

[52] D. Korotkov, "Vagner v Kremle", *Fontanka.ru*, 12 December 2016.
[53] Phoenix, Zhongguo qiye haiwai anquan guanli baogao (International Think Tank Chinese Companies Overseas Security Report), 30 March 2016.

and logistics tasks while retaining the management and communication functions. This outsourcing of the security function is not only driven by the lack of extensive experience in the field, but also by current Chinese laws which forbid Chinese citizens to carry weapons at home or abroad. Exceptions are granted – for example to escorts guarding valuable goods in transit within China or to anti-piracy guards on Chinese merchant shipping – but only in very few cases and under very strict conditions.

Chinese PSCs are already evolving from local security enterprises operating at a municipal level to guard company buildings within China to international companies with intelligence-gathering and high-level security capabilities in dangerous areas far beyond Chinese borders. Chinese state insurance companies wishing to avoid losses on property and life along the BRI are increasingly concerned to promote efficient risk assessment and risk mitigation, and this includes the use and upgrading of PSCs. Beijing's security cooperation with Moscow could also lead to closer cooperation between the Chinese and Russian private security industries.

What Role for the European Union?

The convergence of Chinese and Russian geopolitical, economic and security interests has reached a significant point, but the relationship between Beijing and Moscow has in the past featured cycles of rapprochement and estrangement. The evidence suggests that the current cycle of Sino-Russian rapprochement will last for several years: Beijing's security needs and Moscow economic requirements are converging, even though China currently leads the partnership. Both China and Russia recognise that their strategic partnership, which is grounded in realpolitik, is going to last as long as the convergence of interests is linked to a lasting strategic value rooted in security and economic cooperation. The strategic implications of their shared security interests, from the fight against terrorism to the use and development of efficient and effective private security companies, have already made an impact on the interests of the West in general, and of the US in particular.

From the EU's standpoint, the convergence of Chinese and Russian interests is steadily diminishing the Union's points of entry for more effective security cooperation with China. The EU's normative power to create a code of conduct for PSCs, to implement conflict mitigation measures, and to promote sustainable development could result in closer security cooperation with China along the BRI, and this might also affect the growing presence of Russian PMSCs. Unlike Russia, which thinks of itself as a world power, China is not yet ready to accept an international security role; and this means that the EU still has time to project its values and promote broader cooperation with the aim of avoiding negative spill-overs from the BRI. As the BRI progresses in accordance with President Xi's vision, China is expected to extend its position as a security provider beyond Central and South Asia to the MENA region. Consistent EU engagement with China in the broader sphere of security cooperation without compromising core European values is not expected to undermine US interests. At the same time, a closer security relationship between Brussels and Beijing could create an alternative before the security ties between China and Russia develop into a more structured, and perhaps permanent, form of cooperation.

4. Russia and China: The Progressive Building of a Major Trading Bloc

Alessia Amighini

In the broader context of deepening Russian-Chinese political relations throughout the 1990s, mostly since the start of a "strategic partnership" in 1996, the economic links between the two countries have until very recently been regarded by most as "the weakest link"[1]. Due to widespread fears in Russia that closer economic relations with China might lead to dependence on what was already, in the late 1990s, expected shortly to become the more successful economy, Russian leaders were reluctant to go beyond the limited economic cooperation and trade with China that had been planned by Moscow and Beijing when the Russian Federation was established in 1991. That is why throughout the 1990s bold ambitions on both sides to reach high levels of bilateral trade were for the most part disappointed on every occasion: such trade was smaller in 1999 than in 1992[2].

For nearly three decades since the collapse of the Soviet Union, Russia and China have significantly intensified their economic and trade relations, progressing from a "strategic partnership" to a "treaty of friendship and cooperation" signed in 2001. This has been caused by both domestic and international factors. On the domestic side, Russia has increasingly

---

[1] J. Wilson, "The Weakest Link", in J. Wilson (ed.), *Strategic Partners: Russian-Chinese Relations in the Post-Soviet Era*, London, Routledge, 2015, pp. 61-92.
[2] Ibid., p. 61.

needed to build growth on stronger foundations than its energy exports to the West, which proved an unreliable economic partner when sanctions were applied over Ukraine. This led to major changes in the political priorities of the Russian government, which had until then rebuffed Chinese invitations for fear that greater economic cooperation would work to China's benefit in an unbalanced relationship. Against a backdrop of changing geopolitical circumstances Moscow has steadily shifted its strategic focus from West to East, and in less than a decade the two countries have managed to revitalise their formerly weak and troublesome economic partnership to such an extent that they are now the key players in a recently-formed trading bloc that covers most of the Eurasian continent.

After analysing the volume and structure of the countries' bilateral trade during the 1990s, this chapter will show how they overcame their difficulties and built stronger economic relations during the next decade and especially in its latter half, when bilateral economic ties began to grow stronger following institutional arrangements and agreements that have fostered a steady improvement in economic cooperation and regional integration. Today China and Russia are major economic partners, increasingly linked by trade and investment: in 2017 Chinese-Russian trade rose 20.8% to more than $84 billion, and China had been Russia's biggest trade partner for eight years running[3]. In the first eight months of 2018, according to Chinese customs data, bilateral trade grew at an annual rate of 25.7% – well above the 9.1% growth rate of China's foreign trade as a whole[4].

The economic relations of the two countries, having been stuck in an unproductive framework during Soviet times, were eventually able to escape it as the result of a strong mutual commitment to enhancing bilateral economic cooperation. In addition, important regional cooperation arrangements have been established, in particular the Eurasian Economic Union

---

[3] L. Xia, "Facts & Figures: China-Russia economic ties in fast lane", *Xinhuanet*, 11 September 2018.
[4] Ibid.

(EAEU) which includes Russia, Belarus, Armenia, Kazakhstan and Kyrgyzstan, taking in the whole area between China and the EU, with a population of 183 million, a combined GDP of more than US$4 trillion, and internal trade growing at some 30% a year. Then there is the Shanghai Cooperation Organization (SCO), which has recently added economic cooperation to its previous object of cooperation on security. More recently, various Free Trade Agreements (FTAs) have been signed between the EAEU and a number of European and Asian countries including China, creating a major trading area that extends from East Asia to the borders of Europe and from India to the Arctic.

The chapter will then review the mounting speculation, inspired by the progressive remaking of a Eurasian economic and trade bloc, as to the implications for the EU in terms of its relationships with Russia, with China and with their partner countries, and also the implications for Europe's overall economic and security strategy. The general view, at least until the global financial crisis, was that the world was becoming organised into three main trading regions: Asia, the Americas, and Europe together with Northern Africa, the Middle East and Russia; but international trade has in fact developed in quite a different way. Since the sanctions of 2014 Russia has become more and more deeply intertwined with China, not just through trade, but also through investment, energy, and transport; its relations with China are now much closer than with Europe, historically its main economic partner. Since trade usually brings cooperation and peace (as the history of the EU itself shows), whereas difficult trade relations often lead to greater friction in international affairs (as we see repeatedly as a result of the current US administration's attitudes), the chapter will conclude with some remarks on a major policy priority for the EU: the need to ensure harmonious trading relations with the new Eurasian trading bloc.

Russia and China in the 1990s: Difficult Trade Relations

The trade relationship between the two biggest of the former command economies had been fairly cumbersome ever since the establishment of the Russian Federation, the main reason being that "trade between the Soviet Union and China consisted largely of a protocol trade consisting of bilateral contracts concluded between governmental structures"[5]. These were usually conducted as barter, with little consideration for the nature or degree of complementarity between the two countries' economies, which would naturally have suggested technology, agriculture and energy as areas of mutually beneficial cooperation and trade.

Various other explanations were offered for the difficulty encountered in building stronger economic relations, including the weakness of the Russian economy[6], a lack of structural complementarity, transport bottlenecks and generally poor connections between the two countries, divergences between their policy priorities – and also a certain hostility in Russian perceptions, firstly of the quality of Chinese products (which were indeed initially poor) and secondly of emerging Chinese preponderance that might threaten Russia's economic independence[7].

For all these reasons, bilateral trade between Russia and China remained at very low levels throughout the 1990s and until the early 2000s (Figure 4.1). During those years, Russian trade with China accounted for less than 2% of Russia's total trade. Europe was a bigger partner by far, with over US$44 billion exports in 1995 and over US$72 billion in 2000, as opposed to US$3.5 billion exports to China in 1995 and US$5.2 billion in 2000, according to data from Unctadstat[8]. Moreover,

---

[5] J. Wilson (2015), p. 72.
[6] Ibid., p. 61.
[7] For a detailed history of bilateral economic relations until the early 2000s, see ibid.
[8] https://unctadstat.unctad.org/wds/ReportFolders/reportFolders.aspx

although serious flaws in official trade data make precise calculation impossible, Russia had a trade surplus with China until 2004. The composition of Russian exports to China during the 1990s remained much the same as that of previous decades: fertiliser, polyethylene and telecommunication equipment were the biggest export categories (Figure 4.2). Natural resources (oil and gas) were not yet the most important item in the bilateral trade structure, as they are today.

Fig. 4.1 - Russian-Chinese trade since 1995 ($M)

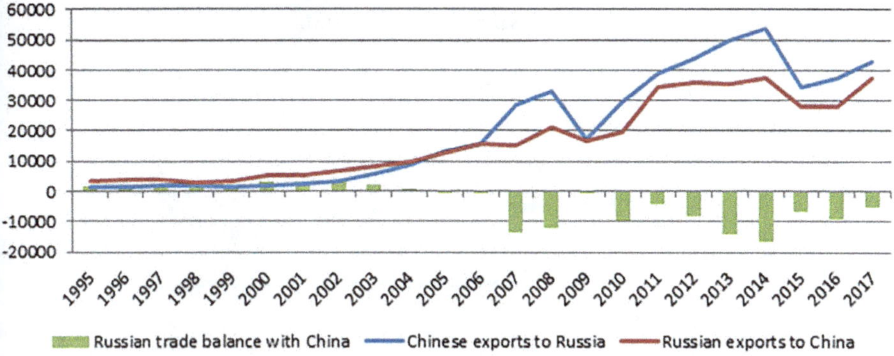

Source: Prepared by the author from data from UnctadStat

Trade between the two countries increased after 2000, and China became an important commercial partner for Russia, which by 2002 was trading more with China than with Italy (once its biggest partner). There was also a significant shift in the bilateral trade balance after 2005, as well as in the composition of their trade. Although the EU as a whole remained the Russia's biggest trading partner (accounting for some US$160 billion or 45% of Russian exports as against 11% to China, and for 36% of Russian imports from the EU as against 21% from China, according to UnctadStat data), Russian-Chinese trade picked up speed in both directions following enhanced cooperation and better connections between the two countries and various institutional arrangements to foster trade links (see below). The structure of Russian exports to China steadily shifted towards energy soon after 2000 as Russia became increasingly dependent on exports of natural resources, especially to China, which was increasingly hungry for secure oil supplies, agricultural goods and semi-finished goods and wanted to benefit from a large neighbouring market for its light manufactures such as clothing, footwear, telecommunication equipment, data processing machinery and electrical appliances (Figure 4.3).

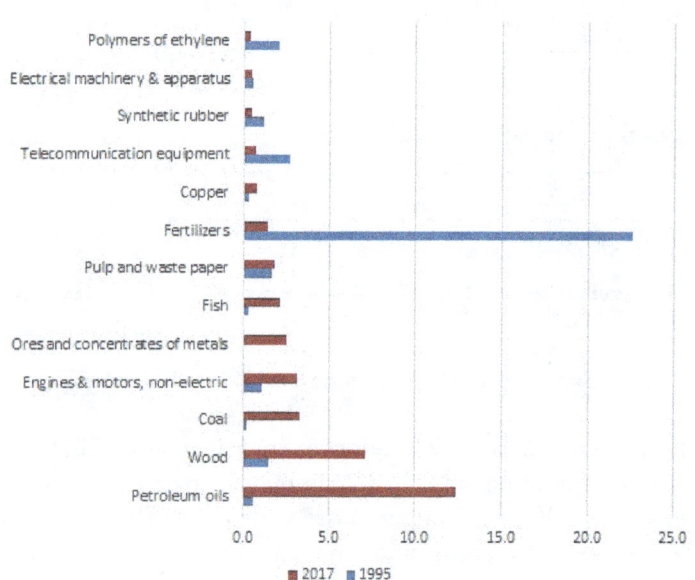

FIG. 4.2 - COMPOSITION OF RUSSIAN EXPORTS TO CHINA, 1995 AND 2017 (% OF TOTAL)

Source: Prepared by the author from UnctadStat data

FIG. 4.3 - COMPOSITION OF RUSSIAN IMPORTS FROM CHINA, 1995 AND 2017 (% OF TOTAL)

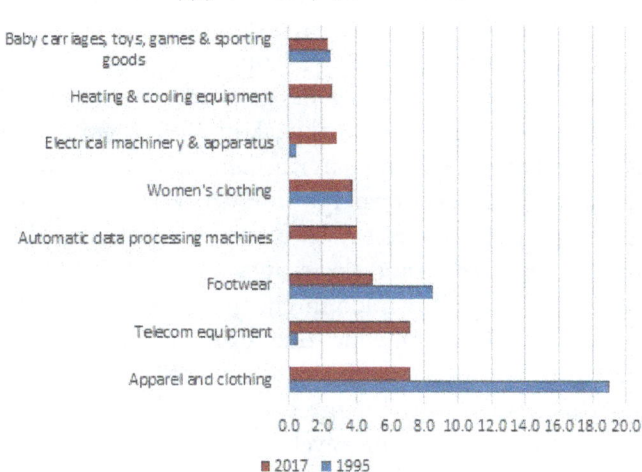

Source: Prepared by the author from UnctadStat data

This structural shift was also the result of increased Chinese investment in energy projects and Chinese stakeholders' acquisition of stakes in big Russian energy companies: Chinese acquisitions in the Russian energy sector were the main vehicle for a convergence of interests in energy cooperation between Moscow and Beijing, and have amounted to more than US$26.5 billion since 2006, more than half of total Chinese direct investment in Russia over the period according to data from the American Enterprise Institute's database "China Global Investment Tracker"[9]). Such cooperation had long been sought by China, but became a reality only when the Russian government found itself in urgent need of a reliable export market with plenty of funding. The process has been summarised as follows: "As Russian resistance to Chinese upstream investments has declined in the aftermath of the post-Ukraine sanctions, Chinese officials have become more interested in opportunities

---

[9] http://www.aei.org/china-global-investment-tracker/

in Russia. Xi explained, "we need to help neighbours in times of crisis [...]. In response, we hope that neighbouring countries will be well inclined towards us, and we hope that our appeal and our influence will grow"[10]. Chinese acquisition of stakes in Russian energy companies has totalled several billion US$ since 2013, reaching an annual peak in 2017 when more than US$5.7 billion were invested in Russian oil and gas businesses[11].

As a result of major energy infrastructure projects bringing gas and power to East Asia, Russia is now China's biggest source of imported oil and electricity and its fifth biggest source of imported coal. This trade in energy will expand further as the Power of Siberia pipeline, due for completion in 2020, is expected to convey up to 38 billion m^3 of natural gas a year from Russia to China. Energy cooperation between the two countries accelerated impressively in 2013, and even more in 2014, as the sanctions imposed on Russia after its invasion of Crimea that year forced its energy export industry to revise its long-term strategy since Europe had starting diversifying its gas suppliers (e.g. in favour of Qatar and the United States) to reduce dependence on Russian sources. Facing Western economic sanctions and with Chinese financial support, Russia launched Novatek's landmark LNG project in the Arctic Yamal Peninsula[12]. Yamal was a first attempt at tapping the huge hydrocarbon reserves in the Arctic and at the same time testing the viability of the northern sea route to China[13]. Yamal LNG, in which the China National Petroleum Corporation and the Silk Road Fund have stakes, began production in December 2017; 54% of its output, according to the Financial Times, is

---

[10] E. Wishnick, "In search of the 'Other' in Asia: Russia-China relations revisited", *The Pacific Review*, 2017, vol. 30, no. 1 , pp. 114-132.
[11] "Russia and China are looking at launching joint projects worth more than $100 billion", *CNBC*, 11 September 2018.
[12] W. Jiang, "Energy Security, Geopolitics and the between China and Russia Gas Deals", *China Brief*, vol. 15, no. 2, 23 January 2015.
[13] H. Foy, "Russia ships first gas from $27bn Arctic project", *Financial Times*, 8 December 2017.

earmarked for China, to which gas can be shipped in about 15 days – roughly half the time taken by the journey via Europe and the Suez canal. In full production LNG shipments to China will be 4m tonnes a year or more. Other agreements include a contract between Russia's state-owned Gazprom and the China National Petroleum Corporation for the construction of a 2,500-mile gas pipeline to China's Heilongjiang province and the deal to bring an additional 30 billion m^3 of gas from western Siberia to China's Xingjian Province for 30 years. Those pipelines together would put China ahead of Germany, Russia's current largest customer.

The early 2000s saw the start of growing trade imbalances between the two countries, in the form of a rising Russian trade deficit *vis-à-vis* China, and a consolidation of the pattern of trade in which Russia mainly supplies natural resources in exchange for manufactured goods. Oil and gas pipelines from Siberia to China have contributed significantly to the shift of bilateral trade towards this energy/manufactures pattern, and accordingly to the growing interdependence between the two economies. This was exactly the form of trade dependence that Russia's earlier leaders had resisted during the 1990s, concerned that it would make Russia increasingly reliant on its natural resources (fuels and minerals account for 63% of Russian exports), to the detriment of its industrial development. Those few manufactured products which Russia exports to China (22% of the total) result from cooperation agreements in the nuclear, aviation and aerospace industries under which Russia has managed to remain a supplier of semi-finished electrical machinery and parts to China. Another area of energy cooperation between China and Russia is nuclear energy: the two countries are to cooperate in developing nuclear power technology: "both countries have signed nuclear deals with Iran, Egypt, Sudan and Turkey, and both have looked to dominate nuclear export markets"[14].

---

[14] S. Reynolds, "Why the civil nuclear trap is part and parcel of the Belt and Road

Some experts regard Russia's recent pivot to Asia[15] and especially towards China as a "strategic necessity" "to ameliorate the economic and demographic situation in the Russian Far East and Eastern Siberia"[16], but also as a broader "opportunity for Russia to break out of the economic, security, and geographic traps she finds herself in within the Western-dominated international order"[17]. Others disagree, however, and emphasise that deeper economic ties between Russia and China could damage Russian industrial development in future. Many commentators see the bilateral relationship between Russia and China as growing constantly closer but at the same time more and more imbalanced, tending to perpetuate the situation where Russia supplies raw materials to China and imports Chinese manufactures. According to this view "Russia should shift the focus of its export policy from negotiating politically driven large projects toward more intensive promotion of consumer goods exports."[18].

Wishnick, though, has recently offered an interesting alternative view of the growing interdependence between Russia and China, arguing that both suffer from resource vulnerabilities and that the widespread notion that increasing economic interdependence favour China rather than Russia might therefore prove somewhat overstated[19]. According to her, "Russia's fears of becoming China's resource appendage are more widely

---

Strategy", *The Diplomat*, 5 July 2018.
[15] F. Hill, B. Lo, "Putin's pivot: why Russia is looking East", *Foreign Affairs*, 31 July 2013; A.C. Kuchins, "Russia's Asia pivot", *Asian Survey*, vol. 54, no. 1, 2014. J.S. Nye, "A new Sino-Russian alliance?", *Project Syndicate*, 12 January 2015; N. Swantsroem, "Sino-Russian relations at the start of the new millennium and beyond", *Journal of Contemporary China*, vol. 23, no. 87, 2014.
[16] M. Bratersky, "Russia's Pivot to Asia: Situational Interest or Strategic Necessity?", *Asian Politics and Policy*, vol. 10, no. 4, 2018, pp. 584-596.
[17] *Ibid.*
[18] I. Makarov, I. Stepanov, and V. Kashin, "Transformation of China's Development Model under Xi Jinping and its Implications for Russian Exports", *Asian Politics & Policy*, vol. 10, no. 4, 2018, pp. 633-654.
[19] E. Wishnick (2017).

discussed than are Chinese insecurities about adequate and secure resource supplies"[20]. The fact is that the two countries have developed a mutual interdependence[21]. China in particular has grown more and more dependent on Russia's resources, not only of oil and gas, but also of water and timber[22].

Oil and gas dependence and the corresponding reliance on energy import routes have been high on the agenda of Chinese policymakers, who have stressed the need to diversify both suppliers and routes. This has made energy cooperation with Russia a high priority for China since the days of Hu Jintao. Russia's position as a major resource supplier to China would appear to compensate for its dependence on Chinese demand. In 2018 Russia may have become China's leading oil supplier, as well as its main supplier of gas.

Water is another resource vulnerability for China, while Russia has abundant and renewable water resources conveniently near its eastern border. What is known as "virtual water", i.e. water used in production processes, is likewise a potential source of dependence on Russia. China is currently the largest importer of Russian timber; and agricultural cooperation, too, has progressed to the extent that China is a big and growing net importer of food; some of the goods on which tariffs have been levied during the current US-China trade war are agricultural products. These forms of resource vulnerability, too, can make China as dependent on its suppliers as they are on China as their main export market.

---

[20] *Ibid.*
[21] H. Zhao, "Does China's rise pose a threat to Russia?", China Institute of International Relations, 26 April 2013.
[22] E.C. Economy, M. Levi, *By All Means Necessary: How China's Resource Quest is Changing the World*, New York, NY, Oxford University Press, 2014.

Improved Connections and Trade Arrangements Since the Early 2000s

Growing economic linkage between Russia and China from the early 2000s benefited from improvements in transport between the two countries, where bottlenecks caused by a severe lack of infrastructure had traditionally been a serious hindrance to trade. New border crossings were opened; air and shipping links proliferated; new railways were built and more communication facilities deployed. But although the two countries share over 4100km of border these areas are relatively inaccessible; the longer, eastern section runs for more than 4000km from the meeting point of China, Mongolia and Russia to that of China, Russia and North Korea just a few kilometres short of the Pacific Ocean; the much shorter western one, less than 100km long, runs in the mostly snow-bound Altai Mountains from western Mongolia to eastern Kazakhstan.

Central Asia remains a very important region for trade between China and Russia because of the difficult geography of their common borders; but Central Asia itself lacks connecting infrastructure as badly as anywhere in the world. World Bank data show that transport costs for many central Asian countries are still extremely high, making imported goods much costlier there than they would be if such infrastructure was adequate. Tajikistan, for example, currently has the highest import costs in the world, at over US$10,000 per container as opposed to a worldwide average of US$1,877[23]. Imports are also very costly in Uzbekistan, one of only two doubly land-locked countries in the world (countries whose neighbours have no direct access to the sea).

The Central Asian countries' combination of rich resource endowments, growth potential and geographical position as a potential bridge from the eastern China to western Russia and

---

[23] N. Hutson, "The Belt and Road through Eurasia: Who Wins and How?", *Eurasianet*, 18 December 2017.

also from China to Europe (two major trading partners) has made Central Asia a policy priority for Beijing since well before the launch of the Belt and Road Initiative in 2013; another geopolitical factor in the region's importance was added in 2001, its proximity to the potential "arc of instability" through Afghanistan, Iran, Pakistan and Iraq[24].

As well as transport connections, Russian-Chinese relations also benefited from effective bilateral mechanisms and agreements and their subsequent institutional development. This major shift in their economic relationship was marked by the arrival on the Russian political scene of Vladimir Putin, who paid more attention to domestic economic interests than Gorbachev in the 1980s. The Putin administration was in favour of large-scale, hi-tech collaborative projects as a means of boosting trade between Russia and China: a 2002 joint communiqué of the two Heads of government said "work should be done to lay a foundation for long-term stability of trade cooperation by increasing the share of high-technology mechanical, electrical and other high value-added products so as to improve the product mix and develop economic ties of advanced forms"[25]. However, it was precisely during those years that the structure of trade between the two countries started to be increasingly biased towards Russian energy exports in exchange for Chinese manufactures, and Russia became increasingly dependent on energy exports. Export concentration increased, and with it trade disparity, developments long resisted by the previous administration. The economic imbalance with China has worsened; China is now Russia's biggest individual trading partner (though not nearly as big as the whole EU); and their bilateral relationship has now become a strategic partnership aimed at counterbalancing the global influence of the United States[26].

Trade development between Russia and China extends well beyond their bilateral links to the broader range of institutional

---

[24] J. Linn, "Central Asia: A New Hub of Global Integration", Brookings, 2007.
[25] J. Wilson (2015), p. 69.
[26] A. Lukin, *China and Russia: The New Rapprochement*, Polity, 2018.

arrangements at supranational or regional level. Russia and China have each originated various trade and cooperation agreements, as each has wanted to manage the process of integrating trade in its neighbourhood, each competing with the other to expand its own area of influence.

First there is the Eurasian Economic Union (EAEU) set up on 1st January 2015 by Russia, Belarus, Kazakhstan, Armenia and Kyrgyzstan. Its combined population is 183m and its total GDP over US$4 trillion; the volume of its internal trade has been growing at around 30% a year. As the EAEU extends as far as the EU (Russia and Belarus border the Baltic states and, most significantly, Poland), it has the potential to disturb or alter the EU's trade with China, and possibly with India and ASEAN as well.

The EAEU may at first sight seem to be a recreation of the old Soviet bloc: member states have a high degree of economic complementarity, and intra-EAEU trade rose 38% in 2016. Unlike the Soviet bloc, however, the region is also very open to external trade. The EAEU's share of total world exports is 3.7%, and its share of world imports is 2.3%. If it were a country its GDP would make it the world's fourth largest economy, just behind Japan but ahead of Germany. Not surprisingly, therefore, many countries have applied for FTAs with the EAEU, among them India, Singapore, Iran and Turkey: forty countries in all are currently involved in FTA negotiations. As we shall shortly see, the union has recently (early 2019) signed an FTA with China; Vietnam is currently the only other Asian state to have an FTA with the EAEU, a deal that has seen Russian investment in Vietnam rise from virtually nil to US$10 billion in just two years[27].

The EAEU is widely regarded as Russia's answer to the EU at a time when the EU has become a more difficult partner due to economic sanctions beginning in 2014; but it should

---

[27] Dezan Shira & Associates, "Vietnam / EAEU FTA Produces US$10 Billion In Russian Investments", *Vietnam Briefing*, 3 July 2019.

also be seen as a Russian reaction to China's increasing pushiness in trying to expand the scope of the SCO, otherwise known as the "Shanghai Pact". The SCO is a Eurasian political, economic and security alliance announced on 15 June 2001 by the leaders of China, Kazakhstan, Kyrgyzstan, Russi a, Tajikistan and Uzbekistan; the SCO Charter formally establishing the organisation was signed in June 2002 and came into force on 19 September 2003. All the founding nations apart from Uzbekistan had previously been members of the Shanghai Five group founded on 26 April 1996. Since 2001 the organisation's membership has expanded to eight countries: India and Pakistan became full members on 9 June 2017 at a summit held in Astana, Kazakhstan. The SCO includes some emerging economies with the most promising potential for growth in the near future such as Pakistan, Uzbekistan and Kazakhstan. Other countries are considering accession: Belarus, Armenia, Vietnam, Iran and Israel. The SCO now accounts for 21% of global GDP, compared with the EU's 22%.

Bilateral ties between China and Russia recently got a major boost from the series of meetings of the Eastern Economic Forum, established by Putin in 2015 and held annually in Vladivostok. In just four years the EEF has become the most important international platform for strategic discussions on developing political, economic and cultural ties between Russia and Pacific Asia.

One major development, the recent EAEU-China FTA, could become a real game-changer not only in regional economic relations but also on a global scale: firstly, the FTA covers countries which together make up by far the greatest part of the Asian-European landmass; secondly, it could overcome the competition between China and Russia to build their own separate spheres of economic and political influence in Central Asia[28].

---

[28] Y. Kim, S. Blank, "Same Bed Different Dreams: China's 'peaceful rise' and Sino-Russian Rivalry in Central Asia", *Journal of Contemporary China* vol. 22, no. 83, 2013; S. Lian 2018, "China and Russia: Collaborators or Competitors?",

The agreement, which is the first major systematic arrangement ever reached between the two groupings, covers thirteen aspects including customs cooperation, trade facilitation, intellectual property rights, industrial cooperation and government procurement, as well as e-commerce and competition. The goal is to reduce non-tariff trade barriers and promote the in-depth development of China's economic and trading relations with the EAEU and its member states. Russia's own trade with China is expected to reach US$100 billion, and the FTA should increase that figure dramatically. The Russian-Chinese trading area is growing faster than China's trade with the EU. Within the EAEU Russia accounts for most of the trade with China, over 85% of exports to China (almost US$33 billion) and over 83% of all imports from China (almost US$45 billion). Other EAEU member states also have valuable economic relations with China (Figure 4.4), but on the investment side rather than in trade.

Commodity turnover between the EAEU countries and China already amounted to more than US$100 billion in 2017, and exports from the EAEU to China rose 40% in that year; so there is already a significant degree of economic integration between China and the EAEU's members, indicating that the recently signed FTA will probably be successful in expanding trade among its members. However, the current structure of trade between EAEU members and China is very similar to that between Russia and China, being largely based on raw material exports from the EAEU in exchange for Chinese manufactures.

Council on Foreign Relations, 2018; N. Chandran, "'Serious' rivalry still drives China-Russia relations despite improving ties", *CNBC*, 14 September 2018; P. Stronski, N. Ng, *Cooperation and Competition: Russia and China in Central Asia, the Russian Far East, and the Arctic*, Carnegie Endowment for International Peace, 28 February 2018.

FIG. 4.4 - TRADE BETWEEN CHINA
AND THE EURASIAN ECONOMIC UNION

Source: Official website of the Eurasian Economic Union, http://www.eaeunion.org/

Growing trade with China over the past decade has further concentrated EAEU members' exports, most notably those of Kazakhstan, Kyrgyzstan and Armenia (Figure 4.5), which is why EAEU members regard export diversification as a fundamental objective in signing the FTA with China.

Cumulative Chinese investment in the countries of the Eurasian Economic Union more than doubled in just six years between 2008 and 2014, from US$11 billion to US$27.1 billion. The main beneficiary of Chinese foreign direct investment (FDI) is not Russia but Kazakhstan, which received almost 90% of the EAEU's cumulative FDI from China, according to data from Chinese Investment Tracker. Chinese investment in Russia has also increased in recent years, however: Chinese direct investment in Russia soared by 72% during the period of negotiations for the FTA between the EAEU and China, reaching US$2.22 billion in 2017.

Fig. 4.5 - Index of export concentration, EAEU members

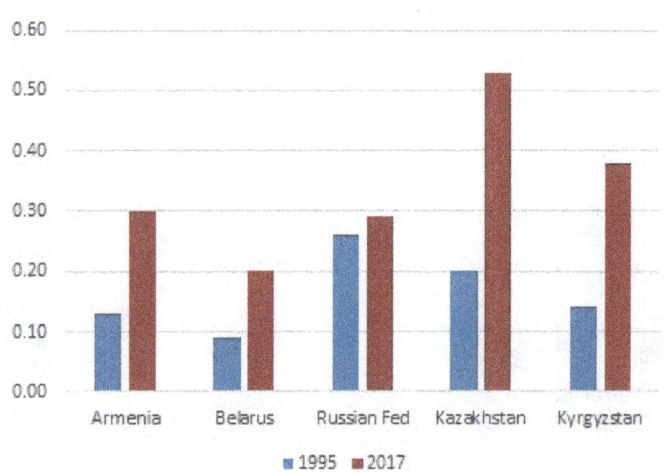

Source: prepared by the author from UnctadStat data

Chinese contractors undertook US$7.75 billion worth of new projects in Russia that year: at 191.4%, the rise in that figure was steeper than those for most countries participating in the Belt and Road Initiative. As a result, China is now the biggest trading partner and source of foreign investment for the Russian Far East. Its FDI mainly takes the form of long-term loans and investments in the minerals/raw materials complex (up to 98% of all investments); but Beijing has also been interested recently in agriculture, and has tried to get Chinese farming companies established in EAEU countries.

The China-EAEU FTA results from a convergence of interests between Russia and China in Central Asia, and potentially also in Southeast Asia. That convergence represents a major shift in Russian foreign policy, in that Moscow's traditional concerns about growing Chinese economic and commercial activities and interests in Central Asia had been exacerbated in 2013 by the announcement in Nursultan (formerly Astana, Kazakhstan) of the Silk Road Economic Belt (SREB), the land-based part of the Belt and Road Initiative (BRI). The convergence has led to the conception and construction of a Greater Eurasian Partnership, a huge economic area stretching across Europe and Asia, which is the ultimate geopolitical ambition of China's Belt and Road Initiative. Its aim is to link Eastern Europe to the eastern and southern areas of Asia by putting together various existing agreements such as the EAEU and the SCO, as well as various corridors such as the Lapis-Lazuli Transit, Trade & Transport Route (also known as the "Lapis Lazuli Corridor"), which connects the Caucasus to Central Asia, and Turkey's Middle Corridor Project (the East-West Trans-Caspian Trade & Transport Corridor). The former starts from Afghanistan, close to the Afghan border where rail connections with Turkmenistan already exist; from there, routes continue west to the Caspian Sea port of Turkmenbashi in Turkmenistan. After crossing the Caspian, the route continues to Baku and Tbilisi, capitals of Azerbaijan and Georgia, and then to the Georgian ports of Poti and Batumi; finally, it will reach Kars and Istanbul in Turkey, at the gates of Europe. Discussions currently under way between the EAEU and Iran, India, Indonesia and Singapore indicate ambitions to extend the Greater Eurasian Partnership to cover the whole ASEAN group, one of whose members (Vietnam) already has an FTA with the EAEU.

Besides connecting the main regions of Asia from North to South and from East to West, China has ambitions for much more diversified ways of connecting to Europe than the present sea routes from southern Chinese ports to the Mediterranean. One major geostrategic goal of the BRI is the Chinese plan to ship goods to Europe via the Northern Passage and the Arctic Ocean, within Russian jurisdiction[29]. Moreover, Kazakhstan, Russia and Belarus are enhancing their routes for rail freight services to Europe, while there are new projects for motorway construction and railroad infrastructure, especially in

---

[29] A. Wong, "China: We are a 'Near-Arctic State' and we want a 'Polar Silk Road'", *CNBC*, 14 February 2018.

Kazakhstan, which is counting on transit revenue of US$5 billion as Chinese goods are carried to and across the European rail network as far as Madrid and London. Overall, the China-EAEU FTA achieves the Chinese goal of traversing the entire Eurasian land mass duty-free as far as the borders of the EU.

Although one of the main aims of the progressive convergence of Russian and Chinese interests in building a greater Eurasian economic area is to link Eurasian economic integration[30] with China's strategic Silk Road Economic Belt project, it is worth noting that the BRI itself could become a source of serious friction in Russian-Chinese relations. At present the BRI involves a multiplicity of trade routes designed to achieve its aim of shipping Chinese exports to Europe, but some experts believe that in order to be economically viable it will eventually have to settle on a single route. This suggests that Russia is actually competing with other member countries of the EAEU to get the maximum benefit from its participation in the BRI, which is one reason why, despite recent signs of cooperation and deepening ties between Russia and China, there remains a degree of "serious geopolitical competition"[31], according to experts including Robert Kaplan of the Center for a New American Security and Dmitri Trenin, Director of the Carnegie Moscow Center. At present one of the main routes preferred by Moscow is the so-called "northern" route relying heavily on Russia's trans-Siberian railway system, but preliminary studies[32] show that a central route – an expanded and upgraded rail network from China's western Xinjiang Province through the Central Asian states, bypassing Russia – is now becoming considerably quicker and cheaper than the trans-Siberian route. This is a source of worry for Russian leaders, for they are increasing their country's links to Asia (and those to China even more) without any certainty as to the net economic benefit for

---

[30] J.F. Linn, *Central Asia: A New Hub of Global Integration*, Brookings, 29 November 2007.
[31] N. Chandran (2018).
[32] N. Hutson (2017).

Russia's domestic economy. Partly to meet their need for product diversification and industrial development, cooperation between China and Russia has recently gained a new momentum, including a joint venture to build wide-bodied long-haul passenger jets (set up in 2017), a research and development centre for high-speed rail technology (last year), field studies and designs for the Moscow-Kazan high-speed railway, and further cooperation in such areas as nuclear power, aerospace, the digital economy and cross-border e-commerce.

Implications for the EU

While discussions about various domestic issues have dominated the debate in Europe, the economic and geopolitical implications of deeper cooperation between Russia and China have been neglected for too long despite their huge potential to affect the future of the EU. European politicians have all underestimated the EAEU as an entity capable of exerting economic influence in the region, unlike the many Asian countries which already joined that union or have expressed an interest in starting negotiations with a view to joining it.

As a matter of fact, a joint initiative, the Eastern Partnership (EaP), was inaugurated by the European Union in Prague back in 2009. It was set up by the European External Action Service together with EU member states and six East European partners to conduct the EU's relationship with the post-Soviet states of Armenia, Azerbaijan, Belarus, Georgia, Moldova and Ukraine, and ultimately to build a common area of democracy, prosperity, stability, and increased cooperation. The EaP has provided a forum for discussions of trade, economic strategy, travel agreements and other issues between the EU and its Eastern European neighbours.

Possibly even more important than the increasing competition around the EU borders, another major implication of closer integration across Eurasia is an emerging competition between the two major Unions – the EU and the EAEU

– for new member countries. Moldova, Ukraine and Georgia have been invited to pursue integration within the EU's EaP and have also been invited to join the Eurasian Economic Union. In 2014, all three countries opted for association agreements with the EU; but breakaway regions of Moldova (Transnistria), Ukraine (Donetsk and Luhansk) and Georgia (South Ossetia and Abkhazia) have expressed a desire to join the Eurasian Customs Union and become part of the Eurasian Economic Union[33].

Pressure has increasingly been applied to the post-Soviet states by both groupings to join their union, especially in 2014 during the tension between Russia and the European Union over the Ukraine conflict. Each side has accused the other of carving out spheres of influence. Members of the EAEU, and Russia in particular, have tried to diversify their trade by signing economic agreements with China, Iran and Turkey. Trade with North and South Korea has also increased.

The recent FTA between the EAEU and the People's Republic of China (the EAEU-China FTA) is a challenge to the EU's position in the world economy, because every new economic agreement has trans-border consequences, especially when it creates a free trade zone of nearly 30m km2 with a population of more than 1.5 billion – and on the EU's doorstep, to boot. The agreement is also an attempt to shift Europe's economic centre of gravity eastwards, and this could exacerbate tension between Brussels and Moscow. In public discourse, policy debates and academic discussions alike, far too little attention has been paid to the re-routing of international trade between China and Europe. Not only will Chinese goods cross the whole of Eurasia without paying any customs duty; Chinese goods can be sent anywhere in the European Union via the main railway route for continental trade through Russia, Belarus and Kazakhstan. What is more, the longest section of border between the two

---

[33] "The New Eurasian Economic Union – A China FTA in the Offing?", *China Briefing*, 9 January 2015.

blocs is that between Belarus and Poland, crossed by the main railway line connecting Berlin and Moscow as well as the European E-30 motorway route. Here, as in all the other areas (in Lithuania and Latvia) around EU-EAEU border crossing points, we may expect a rapid growth in Chinese infrastructure investment, and EU manufacturers, especially SMEs, are likely to face stiffer competition under the new circumstances of trade with the East.

Armenia is an example of EU-EAEU competition not benefiting a third country as it decides to apply for membership of one union or the other. Armenia, which was included in the EaP, opted in 2013 to join the EAEU rather than sign the Association Agreement offered by the EU[34], although the latter would probably have promoted faster social and economic development in the country than membership of the EAEU, where Armenia is not well integrated and is actually falling into greater economic dependence on China.

Another important effect of the EAEU-China FTA is likely to be a change in the traditional areas of cooperation between Russia (and the EAEU) and the European Union. The implications of growing cooperation within Eurasia may affect the strategic agreements on energy between Moscow and Berlin, but their impact may also be felt by the whole EU, which could be obliged to accept a new economic order in Eastern Europe and Asia.

As the United Kingdom leaves the EU and its eastward enlargement comes to a standstill, Brussels should consider enhancing its neighbourhood policy through a Wider European Economic Area (WEEA)[35]. Among other essential ways of strengthening links, the first priority in this WEEA initiative

---

[34] P. De Micco, *When choosing means losing. The Eastern partners, the EU and the Eurasian Economic Union*, Policy Department, Directorate-General for External Policies, March 2015.

[35] As suggested by Michael Emerson, of the Brussels think tank Centre for European Policy Studies: M. Emerson, *The Strategic Potential of the Emerging Wider European Economic Area*, Policy Insights, 5 February 2018.

should be free trade, as currently enjoyed by non-members such as Norway and Switzerland, for countries in the Balkans and Eastern Europe which have association agreements with the EU. The WEEA could become a framework in which the EU could coordinate dealings with the EAEU and China's BRI. This prospect has become particularly important in view of the rapid expansion of China's area of broader economic and political influence in Europe, including the recent move by Greece to join the 16+1 initiative and the signing of Memorandums of Understanding between China and various EU member states – Portugal, Italy and Luxembourg – well beyond the EU's central and eastern regions.

5. The Sino-Russian Challenge to the US Dollar Hegemony

Vasilii Nosov

The question of a scheme by China and Russia to challenge the primacy of the US dollar in international payments has been widely discussed in the media in recent years. In many Western countries rapprochement between China and Russia seems a dramatic challenge to the established international system of neoliberal institutions[1], and every report of another financial or economic agreement reached by Moscow and Beijing becomes an important news story in Europe and the United States. This media attention overlooks the fact that more often than not these agreements are just Memorandums of Understanding, a kind of a non-binding agreement that is no more than an informal step before a contract is signed.

Recently all eyes in the West were on the agreement for a yuan-rouble foreign exchange swap between the People's Bank of China and the Central Bank of the Russian Federation (the two countries' central banks). That agreement marked the launch of a system for cross-border payment in national currencies between China and Russia. The deal was understandably seen as potentially capable of making significant inroads in the proportion of bilateral payments between the two countries settled in USD; but it soon transpired that such expectations were inflated, as most of the arrangements remained ineffective. Russian market

---

[1] J. Anderlini, "China and Russia's dangerous liaison", *Financial Times*, 8 August 2018.

participants regularly stress that cooperation is not as extensive as the countries' leaders proclaim, and accuse Chinese banks of being wary of cooperating with Russian counterparties[2]. Moreover, in late December 2018, China officially declined an intergovernmental agreement to switch to payments in national currencies, an agreement that had been supposed a significant move in the process of de-dollarising Chinese-Russian trade[3]. The rationale for the move would have been greater security for banks financing commercial contracts against the pressure of US sanctions.

Although China's unwillingness to switch looks like an official admission that plans to collaborate with Russia in the financial sphere have failed, there are still obvious reasons for interest on both sides in economic agreements, and the possibility of currency cooperation between Moscow and Beijing in future should not be dismissed. Many economic agreements are indeed being signed at the highest government level, while both China and Russia are experiencing unprecedented tensions with the US, which could create more room for currency cooperation. Nevertheless, each side has its own constraints in proceeding with this kind of partnership, as shown by the fact that the agreements signed remain ineffective.

This chapter will briefly survey the current state of financial cooperation between China and Russia, and will try to make reasonable forecasts about its future prospects. The chapter is structured as follows: first, it outlines the existing financial cooperation arrangements between Russia and China, and the current status of their engagement. Second, it considers the economic and political interests of Beijing and Moscow in financial cooperation. Third, it reviews the current obstacles in the way of developing a financial partnership between the two

---

[2] M. Korostikov, A. Dzhumaylo, K. Dementieva, O. Trutnev, and A. Kostyrev, "Novoye kitayskoye predubezhdeniye" ("New Chinese Prejudice"), *Kommersant*, no. 195, 24 October 2018, p. 1.

[3] "Russia, China Postpone Deal on Yuan-Ruble Settlements – Russian Finance Minister", *Sputnik International*, 25 December 2018.

countries. The conclusion assesses the possibility that collaboration between China and Russia in financial matters could be taken further.

Current Situation

The best-known examples of Chinese-Russian plans for collaboration in financial matters are the agreements on a renminbi-rouble foreign exchange swap. The currency swap line is an instrument which gives each of the central banks of the two countries concerned instant and constant access to a certain amount of the other's currency for it to lend to its own country's commercial banks, so facilitating the provision of finance for foreign trade deals between businesses in the two countries which are signatories to the swap agreement. The China-Russia swap agreement was signed by the Central Bank of the Russian Federation and the People's Bank of China in 2014. They decided on an RMB150 billion (approximately US$25 billion) bilateral currency swap[4]. The agreement was extended at the end of 2017 for another three years on the same conditions.

This arrangement is not China's only one, however: Beijing has such contracts with dozens of countries, and the Russian swap line is by no means the biggest. There are, for example, contracts for RMB360 billion with South Korea, RMB350 billion with the European Central Bank, RMB300 billion with Singapore and the same with the UK, RMB200 billion each with Canada, Australia and Japan, RMB190 billion with Brazil and RMB180 billion with Malaysia. The head of the China branch of the Russian Central Bank, Vladimir Danilov, when attending the forum on "Investment and financial opportunities of the Russian capital market" organised by the Moscow and Shanghai stock exchanges, said that the volume of yuan-rouble swap trades had reached 732 billion roubles (about US$11.6 billion) in January-September of 2018, almost twice as much

---

[4] "In De-dollarization China Trusts", *Sputnik International*, 10 October 2018.

as in the whole of 2017 (about US$6.4 bn)[5]. A similar figure was mentioned by Igor Marich, Managing Director for Money and Derivatives Markets at the Moscow Exchange, who said the trade volume covered by yuan-rouble swaps had been almost 2.5 times larger in January-October 2018 than in 2017[6].

The figures do not seem impressive by comparison with the size of the Russian economy (2018 GDP US$1.65 trillion), still less the Chinese (US$13.25 trillion – these are first estimates from the countries' statistics agencies); but they do represent some 15% of Chinese-Russian trade, which (rising from just US$68 billion in 2014) hit a record high of US$106.6 billion in 2018, 10.8% above the previous year. From the growth in trade one might predict a significant rise in currency swaps in the near future; but there are various reasons to be sceptical.

First of all, optimism concerning the growth of currency swaps between China and Russia could be dented by the fact that the proportion of payments between the two countries settled in roubles or other currencies (including the RMB) fell significantly between Q1 and Q3 of 2018[7]. According to Russian Central Bank data, the proportion settled in US$ reached 89.3% in the second quarter of 2018 (its highest since Q3 2015), and then fell to its lowest level since 2013 (76.5%); but that decline was not to the benefit of settlements in roubles or yuan: the former fell from 10.4% in Q2 2017 to 5.8% in Q2 2018 (its lowest since Q1 2016) and then rose only to 6.1% in the next quarter. The share of all currencies other than the USD, EUR, and RUB fell from 8.4% in Q2 2017 to 3.8% in Q2 2018, its lowest since Q3 2015, and 4.7% the next quarter.

---

[5] "Ob"yem torgov svop-paroy yuan'/rubl' na Mosbirzhe uvelichilsya v yanvare-sentyabre do 732 mlrd rubley" ("Moscow Exchange's yuan-ruble swap trading volume increased in January-September to 732 billion rubles"), *Vesti Finance*, 21 November 2018.

[6] "Rouble and Yuan Challenge US Dollar Hegemony - Financial Experts", *Sputnik International*, 28 November 2018.

[7] Central Bank of Russia, *Valyutnaya struktura raschetov za postavki tovarov i okazaniye uslug po vneshnetorgovym dogovoram* (*Currency structure of settlements for the supply of goods and the provision of services under foreign trade agreements*), 2019.

There was an impressive rise in EUR usage in bilateral payments: it reached 12.7% in Q3 2018, its highest level ever; the previous peak had been just 6.6%, in Q3 2016.

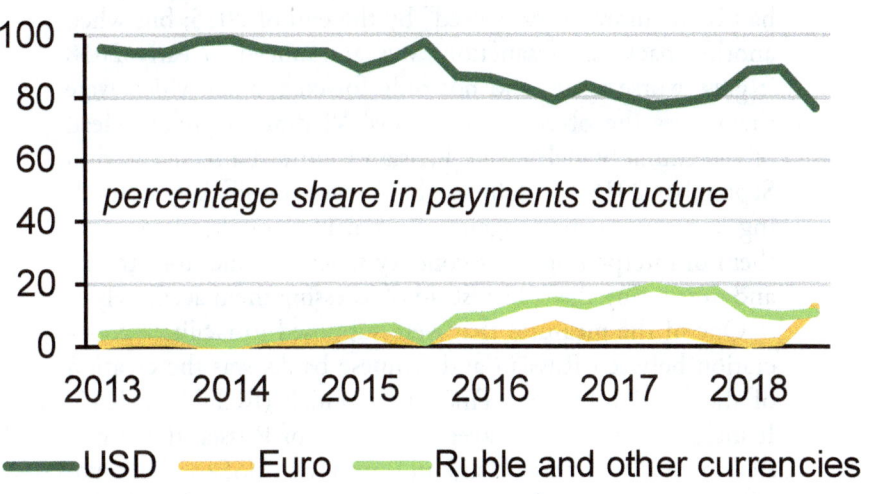

FIG. 5.1 - SETTLEMENTS IN USD, EUR AND OTHER CURRENCIES (INCLUDING RUB) BETWEEN CHINA AND RUSSIA: %

Source: Central Bank of the Russian Federation

Moreover, there were several signs that Chinese banks are not very eager to work with Russia. Russian business leaders reported that Chinese banks had become significantly less willing to help finance foreign trade deals in 2015. Sergey Shvetsov, First Deputy Governor of the Bank of Russia, said in November 2015 that Chinese banks were afraid of falling foul of economic sanctions imposed by Western countries if they cooperated with Russian banks[8]. My sources in the Russian banking industry tell

---

[8] "Banki Kitaya boyatsya rabotat' s RF iz-za sanktsiy SSHA" ("Chinese banks are afraid of cooperation with Russia due to the US sanctions"), *Vesti Finance*, 6 November 2015.

me that Russian banks usually have to make strenuous efforts to convince their Chinese counterparts that a proposed transaction is safe. In October 2018, the story reached Russia's leading media: the Kommersant newspaper published an article on the problems faced by Russian financial institutions in dealing with Chinese banks. Several of the paper's sources stressed that this issue had begun in 2014 after the first wave of sanctions, and had been "more or less solved" by the end of 2015; but when another package of sanctions was announced in early 2018 it grew worse again, and not only for companies which were themselves the object of sanctions. Vladimir Danilov, Head of the China branch of the Russian Central Bank, claimed in September 2018 that Chinese banks were unofficially upholding Western sanctions against Russia. He had already accused them of interpreting the secondary sanctions rules too strictly, and overstating the risks instead of assessing them accurately[9].

One of the measures that were supposed to facilitate cooperation between Russian and Chinese banks was the creation of the Russian-Chinese Financial Council (RCFC) in 2015. It includes two major players: Sberbank of Russia, the largest state-owned commercial bank in Russia with US$465 billion of assets[10], and Harbin Bank, a public commercial bank in China and the country's 28th largest, with US$84 billion of assets[11]. The disproportion between these banks' rankings in their own countries did not itself indicate Chinese lack of interest in setting up the RCFC, for Harbin Bank is the second largest bank in China's North-East, the region most involved in cooperation with Russia. Beside Sberbank and Harbin Bank, almost 70 other banks from the two countries joined the RCFC. Its main objects are to facilitate the financing of foreign trade operations and to promote cooperation between regional banks in

---

[9] "Kommercheskiye banki v KNR 'rasshiritel'no interpretiruyut' sanktsii v otnoshenii Rossii" ("Commercial banks in the PRC interpret sanctions against Russia 'broadly'"), *Kommersant*, 21 November 2018.
[10] Sberbank of Russia, *2017 Annual Report*, 2018, p. 11.
[11] Ernst&Young, *Listed banks in China: 2017 review and outlook*, 2018, p. 20.

Russia and China, especially in the border regions. However, as my Russian banking sources tell me under cover of anonymity, there is none of the deep Chinese-Russian cooperation in the financial sector that was initially expected. For example, not all Chinese RCFC members have opened accounts with Russian banks, indicating that Chinese banks are not really keen to be involved with Russian counterparties.

Even though the Russian-Chinese Financial Council has been in operation for over four years, there have been no announcements in the media of any significant successes. Press reports mostly deal with new arrangements and new Memorandums of Understanding signed during the RCFC's Annual General Meeting. In June 2017, Dmitry Sukhoverov, Head of Sberbank's Far Eastern Russia branch, announced a Memorandum of Understanding between Sberbank and Harbin Bank to create a new investment fund called "Money-Time" with a particular focus on tech start-ups and other innovative companies[12]; but this was the one and only mention of such a fund in the press.

In October 2018, Sergey Gorkov, Deputy Minister of Economic Development of the Russian Federation, announced that Russia and China were planning an intergovernmental agreement to boost the use of national currencies in trade settlements[13]. He said the process was not easy, but stressed that China and Russia had experience of using national currencies in bilateral trade, and pointed to the yuan-rouble foreign exchange swap as an example of cooperation. In November, Igor Shuvalov, Head of the Russian state development bank VEB, briefed the press on the draft agreement that had already been submitted to the Chinese and Russian Prime Ministers: both countries had payment systems; the only issue was to agree on how those systems should cooperate. Shuvalov also said that

---

[12] "Sberbank i Bank Kharbina namereny sozdat' fond v $50 mln dlya investitsiy v startapy" ("Sberbank and Harbin Bank intend to set a $50 mln fund aims to invest in startups"), *TASS*, 19 June 2017.

[13] "Russia & China preparing to ditch dollar for national currencies in trade – top official", *Russia Today*, 18 October 2018.

because China's leader Xi Jinping was taking considerable interest in starting payments in national currencies as soon as possible, the agreement could be signed by the end of 2018. In December, however, the First Deputy Prime Minister of Russia, Anton Siluanov, announced that the signing of the agreement had been postponed[14]; he said it would be signed, but "later, and in another form". The probable reason for China's reluctance to sign the agreement (or even a Memorandum of Understanding) was its desire to avoid sensitive issues during the US-China tariff negotiations, but it could also be illustrating how cooperation with Russia is not a sensible move for China if it results in worsening relations with the United States.

Economic Considerations

Both Russia and China have serious economic reasons for their interest in the development of rouble-yuan FX swaps and other forms of financial cooperation, but the two countries' objectives differ quite significantly. Their primary interest to Russia is as an opportunity of evading financial restrictions imposed by the US and European countries and finding new sources of finance, as well as new markets for Russian companies on the sanctions list[15]. Russian firms worry, though, about the limited prospects for using their RMB in transactions with third parties, since the European companies which have traditionally been their main partners do not usually have a need for Chinese currency. Because RMB is not freely convertible, the only real possibility of using such these funds is in deals with Chinese companies, but there are no ties with such firms sufficient to enable Russian companies to give up their European counterparties and replace them with Chinese ones.

---

[14] "Rouble and Yuan Challenge US Dollar Hegemony - Financial Experts"…, cit.
[15] I. Ivory, "Why Russia's pivot East is crucial for its own survival", *CNBC*, 27 January 2016.

Several projects based on Sino-Russian collaboration exist only on paper. One of the most telling examples is the Moscow-Kazan high-speed railway, an agreement the signed by Russian Railways and the China Railway Eryuan Engineering Group during a meeting between Putin and Xi Jinping on a visit to Moscow. The 772-kilometre high-speed railway was supposed to link Moscow and Kazan. The project's main interest for the Chinese was the opportunity to include this route in an ambitious project for a Beijing – Moscow railway, regarded as part of the Belt and Road railway system[16]. Several agreements were signed, most of them in the form of Memorandums of Understanding. Moscow expected to receive substantial support from China for the project, but Beijing wanted it to have Russian state guarantees. When China asked for them, the Russian side demurred on the grounds that the concession agreement itself already provided guarantees. In May 2016, the Russian media reported that China had agreed to provide financing (400 billion roubles, about US$6 billion) without demanding government guarantees[17]; but thereafter China lost interest in the project. There were reports of European investors seeking to participate in the Moscow-Kazan high-speed railway, the latest being a Memorandum of Understanding between the government of the Russian Republic of Tatarstan and a number of Italian companies[18], but this Memorandum of Understanding has still failed to produce a real contract.

According to Russian media reports, in January 2019 a decision had been taken to build the first section of the line, from

---

[16] The Belt and Road Initiative is the core Chinese geopolitical project of 2010s, aimed at the infrastructural development of Asia that would connect all countries in the region and link China with Europe. For a more detailed analysis on the BRI, see chapter 3 in this volume.

[17] N. Skorlygina, A. Vedeneeva, "Kitaytsev ostavili bez gosgarantiy po VSM" ("The Chinese have been left without state guarantees for the High-Speed Railway"), *Kommersant*, no. 90, 25 May 2016, p. 7.

[18] "Buon viaggio: Russian high-speed railway project attracts another European investor", *Russia Today*, 23 March 2018.

Moscow to Nizhny Novgorod[19], at an estimated cost of 621 billion roubles (almost US$10 billion), 200 billion of which would be met out of government funds, 200 billion would come from Russian Railways (the railway monopoly), and another 220 billion from a concession-holder. Unfortunately, there has still been no decision as to who that concessionaire should be: the news mentioned possible German and Chinese candidates. To judge by the record of previous agreements with Chinese investors, final approval and financing from China could take a long time. Moreover, in December 2018 Maxim Oreshkin, Russian Minister for Economic Development[20], and Anton Siluanov, First Deputy Prime Minister and former Finance Minister of the Russian Federation, cast doubts on the project's economic viability[21]. So, unless there is a decisive breakthrough in negotiations with foreign investors, this project will probably be postponed.

China now has two significant reasons to be interested in promoting financial cooperation, and the yuan-rouble foreign exchange swap in particular. First, internationalisation of the renminbi and an increase in the proportion of global settlements conducted in the currency are two of the Chinese government's main policy goals, and the financing of commercial contracts with Russia in RMB helps towards achieving them. The most reliable source for currency settlement totals is the Triennial Central Bank Survey published by the Bank for International Settlements, the oldest of the global financial institutions, whose primary purpose is to assist central banks'

---

[19] N. Skorlygina, "Odobren pervyy uchastok vysokoskorostnoy zheleznodorozhnoy magistral" ("The first section of the High-Speed Railway has been approved"), *Kommersant*, no. 9, 21 January 2019.

[20] D. Makarova, "Maksim Oreshkin usomnilsya v sotsial'no-ekonomicheskoy effektivnosti VSM Moskva – Kazan" ("Maxim Oreshkin doubted the socio-economic efficiency of the Moscow-Kazan High-Speed Railway"), *Kommersant*, 12 December 2018.

[21] "Siluanov raskritikoval proyekt vysokoskorostnoy magistrali Moskva – Kazan" ("Siluanov criticized the project of the Moscow - Kazan High-Speed Railway"), *Vedomosti*, 25 December 2018.

efforts to maintain monetary and financial stability. The Survey is published every three years, and the latest survey was released in December 2016[22]. According to that survey, the percentage of total global settlements made in RMB had almost doubled since 2013, and reached 4% (out of 200%, due to double counting). The inclusion in January 2016 of RMB in the basket of currencies making up Special Drawing Rights (SDRs, the supplementary foreign-exchange reserve assets defined and maintained by the International Monetary Fund) has had some influence, but it seems impossible to quantify the direct impact of the change. China's involvement in big infrastructure projects in Africa (such as African railway construction by the China Road and Bridge Corporation, one of the world's largest infrastructure companies, with Chinese finance) may also be affecting the increase in RMB settlements worldwide: according to data from the China Africa Research Initiative (CARI) at the Johns Hopkins University School of Advanced International Studies, total lending from China to Africa in 2000-2017 exceeded US$143 billion[23] and, as Deborah Brautigam and Jyhjong Hwang from CARI point out, loans provided by the Chinese Ministry of Commerce and Eximbank are always denominated in RMB[24]. But since there are no official Chinese data on loans to Africa, it would seem impossible to provide any clear estimate of such lending's contribution to the rise in worldwide RMB settlements.

As for the use of the rouble for payments within China, or between China and third countries, it does not seem realistic in view of low demand for the rouble internationally. This is

---

[22] Bank for International Settlements, *Triennial Central Bank Survey. Global foreign exchange market turnover in 2016*, Monetary and Economic Department, 2016, p. 72.

[23] China Africa Research Initiative, "Data: Chinese loans to Africa", Johns Hopkins. School of Advanced International Studies, 2018.

[24] D. Brautigam, J. Hwang, *China-Africa loan database research guidebook*, China Africa Research Initiative, Johns Hopkins School of Advanced International Studies, 2016.

the most important reason for Chinese firms' lack of interest in implementing the yuan-rouble swap. Moreover, using a significant amount of Russian currency in payments goes against the policy of raising the RMB's share in global settlements, and that too lessens China's interest in it. Interest in promoting bilateral FX swaps is therefore significantly limited in both countries, and even if the rouble becomes a freely convertible currency the lack of demand for it will still restrict its use.

The second reason for China to be interested in implementing such a financial instrument would be to make it easier for China's banks and firms to finance Chinese-Russian commercial contracts. According to the statistics, the volume of trade between Russia and China has significantly increased in recent years: the total rose from US$70 billion in 2016 to US$107 billion in 2018[25]. The main driver of this growth has been the rapid rise in oil prices and China's growing demand for oil, natural gas, timber and metals. Due to the increase in China's oil and gas consumption and the corresponding demand for imports, we may expect further growth in the years to come (at least in quantity), but no significant breakthrough is expected in other goods. From 2014 to 2018, China's imports excluding mineral products rose from US$11 billion to US$15 billion, but the value of China's imports of mineral products fell over those years (from US$31 billion in 2014 to US$21 billion in 2015 and US$20 billion in 2016) as a result of the fall in prices of energy resources (the Urals oil price went down from an average of US$97.8 per barrel in 2014 to US$51.4 per barrel in 2015 and US$42.1 per barrel in 2016). In 2018, after the oil price had risen to an average of US$69.9 per barrel (its highest level since 2014), the value of China's mineral imports increased from US$28 billion in 2017 to US$43 billion in 2018[26]. Based on these figures and the limited interest of Chinese companies in trading with Russia, there is no reason

---

[25] General Administration of Customs People's Republic of China, "Imports and Exports by Country (Region) of Origin/Destination", December 2018.
[26] *Ibid.*

to expect any sizeable increase in volumes of trade in any sector other than energy resources, and therefore little reason for any further development of yuan-rouble swaps or the cross-border payments system generally.

FIG. 5.2 - TOTAL CHINESE-RUSSIAN TRADE LARGELY DEPENDS ON THE VALUE OF CHINA'S MINERAL IMPORTS

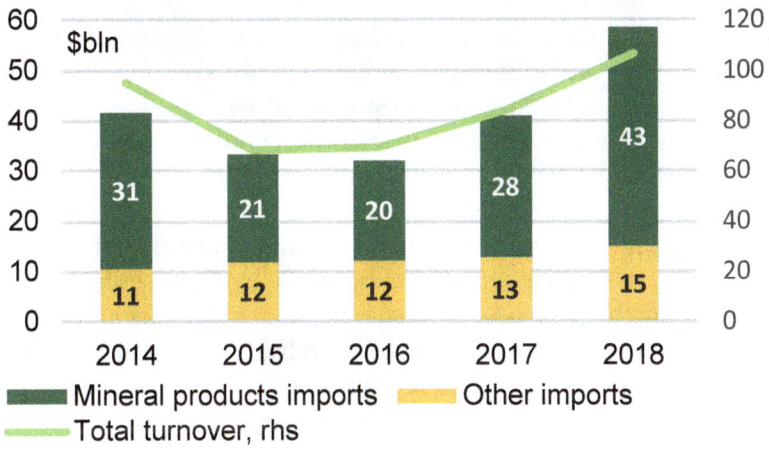

Source: General Customs Administration of China

In March 2018, the Shanghai International Energy Exchange (INE) launched yuan-denominated oil futures, or "petroyuans" (as opposed to "petrodollars"). Since China is the largest oil importer in the world, this was a reasonable attempt to lure oil traders away from Western markets (for example, Russian oil companies under sanctions, including the state-led group Rosneft). In December 2018, daily trading volume exceeded 500,000 contracts (1,000 barrels per contract) and accounted for nearly half of WTI oil trade volumes[27]; but it is too soon to say whether the petroyuan is becoming a new oil benchmark,

---

[27] Y. Cho, T. Kumon, "China, Russia and EU edge away from petrodollar", *Nikkei Asian Review*, 7 January 2019.

even in the Asian region. China has a long record of dramatic upticks in its markets, and the present case looks similar. The best-known example is a bubble that developed in 2014-2015 on the Shanghai and Shenzhen stock markets when they were first opened to individual investors[28]; but the biggest of all, though barely noticed at the time because all eyes were on the stock markets, was an attempt to launch yuan-denominated metal futures in 2015. Within six weeks of the launch, the volumes of trades outstripped the London Metal Exchange. Garry Jones, the Head of the LME at that time, observed that most of the Shanghai-based traders probably did not even know what exactly they were trading[29]. Fuel brokers say the situation today feels similar, and that most investors in Shanghai crude oil futures are Chinese individuals who do not monitor or heed market fundamentals[30]. In view of this, it is plausible that the growth in trading volume has been due by Chinese investors reselling the same assets to each other, something that may well deter foreign investors who would probably prefer Western oil exchanges with reasonable dynamics based on market fundamentals. Moreover, foreign investors may feel a lack of confidence in RMB as an investment currency. China's launch of yuan-denominated oil futures is therefore unlikely to lead to competition between the yuan and the dollar in the crude oil market any time soon.

Political Considerations

Although negotiations are constantly going on between Chinese and Russian official bodies or companies, almost all agreements

---

[28] A. Swanson, "China stock market: Five facts that show how the bubble arose - and why it might be bursting", *Independent*, 26 June 2015.
[29] J. Ng, "LME Head Says China Traders Don't Know What They Buy in Boom", *Bloomberg*, 27 April 2016.
[30] H. Gloystein, "China's flawed futures contract pushes oil trade to record high in 2018", *Reuters*, 12 December 2018.

between the two sides have been signed during meetings of the top policymakers: the Chinese and Russian Presidents Xi Jinping and Vladimir Putin, or their Prime Ministers Li Keqiang and Dmitry Medvedev. This may be taken as a sign that businesses in the two countries find themselves unable to finalise agreements on the basis of commercial profitability. On the other hand, the signing of agreements amounting to billions of US$ based on the two governments' political interests may well be an indicator of their ongoing rapprochement, which brings them political advantages both domestically and internationally. Chinese and Russian firms, especially state-owned businesses, cannot get out of making such agreements even if they foresee little profit from them. This difference between political and economic calculations results in the signing of plenty of Memorandums of Understanding, for they can be presented as significant political achievements but do not oblige companies to cooperate. Thus the political will of the countries' leaders is a necessary condition for cooperation between China and Russia; but the practical business of cooperation also requires constant effort, not sporadic meetings of top officials. This mismatch in the interests of political and business leaders in both countries partly explains why most of the agreements have not been implemented in full, even after several years.

The political reasons for such close relations between Xi and Putin may be divided into two main categories, internal and external. China is striving to become a new superpower, and Russia considers itself a superpower still. For the citizens of both countries, cooperation between China and Russia can be taken as a sign of growing influence on the world stage and as a source of reassurance, particularly at times of acute tension with the Western world as represented by the United States and, to some extent, Europe.

Both China and Russia also have local geopolitical conflicts for which they are regularly criticised by Western countries, and each needs the other's support in international organisations. Far from joining in Western condemnation of Russia's annexation of Crimea, China emphasised that it understands the challenges and threats faced by Russia over Ukraine and supports Moscow's approach to the settlement of the issue[31]. Conversely, in connection with tension over the South China Sea, the Russian Foreign Minister Sergey Lavrov declared in April 2016 that such disputes should be settled by the states involved without interference from third countries[32]. Though there are other countries which support China and Russia in the United Nations, each is certainly the other's most influential partner since both are permanent members of the Security Council, the most powerful body in the United. In terms of geopolitics, it undoubtedly is a mutually beneficial partnership.

Future Prospects

As explained above, the main obstacle to the development of financial cooperation between China and Russia and to their plans to challenge the hegemony of the US dollar is the mismatch between the political desire for mutual accommodation and the real economic costs and benefits. Dozens of agreements are signed by Russian and Chinese companies and government bodies during meetings between the two countries' leaders or prime ministers, but the recent record gives no grounds for expecting any breakthrough in cooperation.

Chinese and Russian leaders have repeatedly claimed that the value of trade between their countries is growing fast; and indeed it has increased from US$70 billion in 2016 to US$107 billion in 2018 (according to the Chinese General Customs Administration)[33]. Such growth rates are impressive, but the reason for them is not closer cooperation. US$27 billion of that

---

[31] "China against declaration of independence at referendums", TASS Russian News Agency, 21 November 2014.
[32] A. Tsvetov, "Did Russia Just Side With China on the South China Sea?", *The Diplomat*, 21 April 2016.
[33] "Imports and Exports by Country (Region) of Origin/Destination"…, cit.

US$37 billion growth is contributed by China's imports, while the contribution of Russia' imports is US$10 billion; and almost 90% (US$24 bn) of that US$27 billion growth in China's figure is accounted for by increased imports of mineral products (oil and other mineral fuels and distillation products, etc.)[34].

The main factor in that significant increase in China's fuel imports from Russia was not a rise in quantity but the worldwide rise in oil prices: in 2016 the yearly average price of Urals oil was US$42.06 per barrel (Reuters data); two years later, the 2018 average was 66% higher, at US$69.90. The rise in the physical quantity of China's oil imports was rather modest, hardly above the roughly 10% annual trend of recent times[35]. According to the International Energy Agency's five-year forecast issued in 2018, China's demand for oil is expected to grow negligibly between 2018 and 2023, at some 0.3% a year[36]. There is little reason to expect China's oil imports from Russia to grow significantly in quantity, and their value will mainly depend on the price of oil.

Construction of the "Power of Siberia" natural gas pipeline should be complete at the end of 2019. The project was signed off in May 2014, when it was claimed that the value of the contract would be as high as US$400 billion over 30 years[37]; but in 2015 global energy prices dropped, raising doubts as to whether the terms of the agreement would be maintained. We may expect further negotiations in the second half of 2019, just before the pipeline's completion, as none have been held to date.

China is certainly interested in importing natural gas because the 13th Five-year-plan (2016-2020) sets a target of 10% for

---

[34] General Administration of Customs People's Republic of China, "Imports by Selected Countries (Regions) and by HS Divisions", December 2018.
[35] General Administration of Customs of People's Republic of China, "Major Import Commodities in Quantity and Value", December 2018.
[36] International Energy Agency, *Oil 2018. Analyses and Forecasts to 2023*, Market Report Series Oil, 2018.
[37] "Russia signs 30-year deal worth $400bn to deliver gas to China", *The Guardian*, 21 May 2014.

the share of natural gas in the fuel mix (it was 6% in 2015)[38]. To reach that target there will have to be a considerable rise in natural gas imports, so the "Power of Siberia" pipeline is expected to go into service, but it is reasonable to anticipate a new round of negotiations in which the gas price could be revised.

In February 2019, a Bill for new sanctions against Russia was introduced in the United States Senate [39]. It does not directly hit Russia's financial sector, but could be a disturbing new signal for Chinese banks and other companies, and may well increase their anxieties about the possible consequences of dealing with Russian firms. Vladimir Danilov, the Head of the China branch of the Russian Central Bank, has warned that the Chinese might significantly downgrade ties with Russian firms without checking for sanctions in each particular case. If future sanctions were to hit the Russian energy sector, it would be difficult for China to give up trading with Russia because it would then have to look for new sources in other countries; but Chinese business would probably distance itself from participation in natural gas projects – such as "Power of Siberia" and "Yamal LNG" – that China had invested in. We may at least be sure that China would forgo further investment in such projects in order to avoid the risk of possible secondary sanctions imposed by the United States.

One of the ways in which China could react to severe sanctions against dealing with Russia could be to set up a financial institution dedicated to providing finance for Chinese-Russian trade. China already has experience of this: there are two banks in China whose only business is to provide funding for trade between China and the Democratic People's Republic of Korea (Bank of Dandong) and between China and Iran (Bank of Kunlun). The Bank of Kunlun is a financial subsidiary of the China National Petroleum Company (CNPC), one of the core

---

[38] Mitsui Global Strategic Studies Institute, *China's energy policy and related issues towards 2020*, 2017, p. 1.
[39] The U.S. Congress, "S.482 - Defending American Security from Kremlin Aggression Act of 2019", 13 February 2019.

investors in the "Yamal LNG" project[40]. This shows that in the event of severe US sanctions on the Russian energy sector, China already has a proven method of getting around them or at least minimising the damage; and the effectiveness of that method was indirectly confirmed by the European Union's High Representative, Federica Mogherini, when she said in December 2018 that the EU would establish a mechanism to facilitate non-dollar transactions with Iran in the near future so as to circumvent US sanctions against Tehran[41]. China, though, would use such a tool only for essential resources like oil and natural gas. As for financial cooperation itself, the most likely scenario is that Chinese banks and other financial institutions will remain very cautious, an attitude usually regarded by Russian government institutions as "unofficially joining in US sanctions".

Conclusion

The possibility of the RMB's potential challenge to the hegemony of the US dollar (with or without Russia's collaboration) is a current talking point in the media and among experts worldwide. It is understandable that economic and political partnership between China and Russia, two permanent members of the United Nations Security Council, is making headlines; but the goal of challenging the US dollar's hegemony does not seem within China's reach in the near future. Cooperation with Russia is unlikely to have a significant impact on the growth of the RMB's share in global settlements because of the limited opportunities for increased economic cooperation – although such cooperation is still in the best interests of both governments.

---

[40] C. Aizhu, "China National Petroleum Corp may cut Kunlun bank's ties to Iran: sources", *Reuters*, 21 December 2018.
[41] V. Dendrinou, N. Chrysoloras, "EU, China, Russia Defy Trump With Plan to Keep Trading With Iran", *Bloomberg*, 25 September 2018.

Furthermore, China faces the problem of insufficient interest in its currency on the part of foreign investors. The case of the "petroyuan" shows how Chinese speculators' neglect of fundamentals affect the dynamics of Chinese securities markets and could seriously discourage potential investors. Talk about whether or not the People's Bank of China manipulates the country's currency also generates additional uncertainty and makes it harder to forecast future fluctuations in the RMB exchange rate. Both factors make the RMB less attractive, and thereby support the leading role of the USD in the financial markets.

Federica Mogherini's prospected special purpose vehicle for payments in France, Britain, Germany, Russia and China to facilitate economic dealings with Iran could be a first step towards developing a new settlements system for those countries. The European Union and China both have to deal with the possible extension of US sanctions to the Russian energy sector. Moreover, the ongoing US-China trade war also poses risks to the European Union's long-term cooperation with China. Steps taken by the US in that quarrel are designed not only to cut the US-China trade deficit but also to hold back China's technological development, one of the key priorities in its strategic plan known as "Made in China 2025". Two of China's ICT manufacturers, ZTE and Huawei, have already been hit by US penalties which, though officially imposed as punishment for breaching sanctions against Iran and North Korea, could also relate indirectly to US-China quarrels over technology: Washington regularly accuses Beijing of intellectual property theft[42], and there is no sign it will relax its pressure on China.

Both China and Russia are important trade partners for the EU. In 2017, according to official statistics provided by the European Commission, China and Russia together accounted for 28% of EU imports (China 20.2% and Russia 7.8%) and

---

[42] S. Pham, "How much has the US lost from China's IP theft?", *CNN Business*, 23 March 2018.

15.1% of EU exports (China 10.5% and Russia 4.6%)[43]. The risk of extended US sanctions against China and Russia could lead the EU, China and Russia to set up new mechanisms of cooperation. It is true that not even the creation of Federica Mogherini's special purpose vehicle would stop the US applying secondary sanctions against European countries; but the setting up of new, independent financial mechanisms for the EU, China and Russia could lay the groundwork for closer cooperation among them in future.

[43] European Commission, Directorate General for Trade, "Client and Supplier Countries of the EU28 in Merchandise Trade", 2018.

Policy Recommendations for the EU
Aldo Ferrari, Eleonora Tafuro Ambrosetti

The "Russia-China bloc" may be described as merely pragmatic, asymmetrical or even at times prone to conflict, but it is here to stay. The one thing all the authors of this report seem to agree on is that Sino-Russian economic, political and (partly) normative convergence is a trend which can expected to continue or strengthen, at least in the short -to-medium term. This is not good news for the EU: Sino-Russian convergence, which is partly driven by both countries' quarrels with the West, further establishes an axis of growing dissent from and competition with the West. That said, rather than overdramatizing this development the EU should look for possible benefits from increased Sino-Russian cooperation – or at least for ways of limiting the damage. Drawing upon the authors' contributions to this Report, we have compiled a few takeaway messages for the EU.

Change Starts at Home

Sino-Russian convergence poses problems for Brussels, especially in the realm of values. While Russia and China do not seem to be actively promoting authoritarianism they do offer alternative models and so implicitly challenge the liberal-democratic narrative; and the EU, which promotes that narrative, has lately increased its warnings about the perils of such alternative models[1]. Russia and China champion conservative "homegrown" values against what they portray as the West's normative imperialism. When China offers money with "no strings attached" as development aid or foreign investment, this diminishes the appeal and leverage of EU schemes and their attendant conditions – although a better understanding of the debt trap is shifting the EU's thinking towards a more structured and transparent investment system. Here the best thing the EU can do is to keep working to make its own liberal-democratic model more consistent and more attractive. First, it must be more consistent: credibility is a scarce resource in international relations, and one of the most successful strategies used by Russia and (to a lesser extent) China is to call out inconsistent Western policies and double standards – something Russia pundits often call "whataboutism", meaning the rhetorical technique of responding to an accusation by making a counter-accusation or raising a different question. Russian president Vladimir Putin and foreign minister Sergey Lavrov have often condemned the EU's double standards in several international crises, from the military intervention against Serbia and recognition of Kosovo's independence by many EU countries to recent actions in Libya. This discourse resonates in other states whose relations with the EU are increasingly difficult. The EU's management of migration and refugees, for instance, exposed some of the EU's inconsistencies and damaged Brussels' reputation as an ethical actor, especially in the eyes of states disproportionately affected by the refugee crisis, such as Turkey. To be fair, the EU's policy-making process is far more complex than that of individual countries; but as Brussels has long boasted of an ethical foreign policy it needs to keep its political actions better aligned with its values.

Secondly, to be more attractive the European model has to work and deliver. While a full recovery from the 2008 financial crisis is still under way, many European citizens feel that they

---

[1] https://ec.europa.eu/commission/sites/beta-political/files/communication-eu-china-a-strategic-outlook.pdf

are bearing the brunt of that crisis, a feeling that many populist parties exploit. The more clearly the EU's neighbours see that the EU model can lead to economic wellbeing and a fairer society, the more attractive they will find it and the more willing they will be to adopt its standards. Unfortunately, the recent slowdown of the EU economy does play into the hands of states providing alternative economic models and policies.

Act Collectively

Divergences in how to manage relations with China and Russia are testing the unity of EU foreign policy, creating or deepening rifts within the EU28. Recent events illustrate this: not only is the Russian-backed Nord Stream 2 pipeline project straining relations between the EU and the US, but it is also becoming a divisive issue within the EU. So is the progress of China's Belt and Road Initiative (BRI) in Europe, as shown by the storm over Italy's endorsement of the initiative. Yet neither the EU nor any of its member states can effectively pursue its objectives concerning China or Russia except through a multilateral approach. When dealing with those countries EU members should ensure that their actions are compatible with EU law and policy, whether they act individually or in sub-regional groups such as the new 17+1 format (Greece became a member in April 2019). The Commission's proposal in 2017 for a regulation establishing a "legal framework for the screening of foreign direct investments (FDI) inflows into the EU" is a step in the right direction, but more needs to be done to ensure that foreign investments are consistent with the EU's *acquis*, and in particular with its environmental standards and its rules on corruption, fair competition and workers' rights. In the case of many EU candidate countries or potential candidates with credible prospects of membership (mostly in the Western Balkans), the EU still has the political leverage to insist that they abide by EU values and standards; but at the same time, given those countries' development needs, the EU should make an effort to further scale-up infrastructure projects to counter China's growing presence in the EU's neighbourhood, while offering them a clear and realistic pathway to membership.

Talk Security, Not Just Business, with China

In terms of security, the convergence of Chinese and Russian interests is steadily reducing the EU's opportunities for more effective security cooperation with China. Unlike Russia, which thinks of itself as a world power, China is still defining its international security role. As the BRI progresses in accordance with President Xi's vision, China is expected to extend its position as a security provider beyond Central and South Asia to the MENA region. While this diminishes the EU's ability to project its own values, Brussels still needs to promote broader cooperation and avoid any potential damage resulting from the BRI. As the EU engages with China in the broader sphere of security cooperation there must be consistency without compromise over core European values. For example, the EU could use its standard-setting powers to introduce a code of conduct for Chinese Private Security Companies (PSCs) protecting Chinese BRI investments, to implement conflict mitigation measures, and to promote sustainable development; this, in turn, would affect the growing presence of Russian PSCs along the BRI. Enhanced EU-China security cooperation could put greater emphasis on the objectives of "peace and security" in the EU-China 2020 Strategic Agenda for Cooperation[2] agreed in 2013 by Brussels and Beijing. That would also be in line with US interests, given that a closer security relationship between Brussels and Beijing could give China an alternative before its security ties with Russia develop further and perhaps result in a military alliance.

---

[2] https://eeas.europa.eu/delegations/china_en/15398/EU-China%202020%20Strategic%20Agenda%20for%20Cooperation

Explore New Forms of Financial Cooperation

Donald Trump's policies are pushing China and Russia closer together; will some of his policies lead to a convergence between Moscow, Beijing and Brussels as well? The EU's opposition to US sanctions on Iran is a case in point: in January 2019 France, Germany and the United Kingdom set up an Instrument in Support of Trade Exchanges (INSTEX) as a "special purpose vehicle" to ensure smoother financial transactions in euros with Iran, better protected from US sanctions. China and Russia are still important trade partners for the EU; the risk of extended US sanctions against China and Russia (beyond those linked to the Ukraine crisis, for which the EU has imposed its own sanctions against Moscow) could lead the EU, China and Russia to set up new cooperation mechanisms like INSTEX. While it is still unclear whether INSTEX will be successful and whether the existence of such a mechanism will suffice to protect European companies from the potential fallout of US secondary sanctions, this example could lay the groundwork for closer cooperation among the EU, China and Russia in future against US policies which all three actors perceive as damaging.

Time To Take the Eurasian Economic Union Seriously

Both China and Russia consider Eurasia their own backyard, and each tries to strengthen its influence there through ambitious regional integration or cooperation initiatives: in Russia's case, the Eurasian Economic Union (EAEU) and the Greater Eurasian Partnership, and in China's the Silk Road Economic Belt, the land component of the BRI. Many analysts see these projects as mutual competitors, but this is not necessarily the case. China and Russia seem to be increasingly in agreement when it comes to the future regional order in Eurasia, and they have enhanced mutual cooperation by linking the EAEU and BRI. A case in point is their division of labour within the Shanghai Cooperation Organisation (SCO), where China is in charge of the economic sphere while Russia takes the lead on security issues; and that division of labour is also apparent within the BRI, as many of the private security companies enlisted in BRI projects are Russian. This may give the EAEU new economic and political importance; for despite its limited economic benefits, membership may bring political advantages as it strengthens the negotiating position of countries like Kyrgyzstan, or even larger Kazakhstan, in the face of overbearing Chinese pressure. EU officials should monitor these developments closely and find ways to engage with the EAEU. This might also ease geopolitical confrontation on the EU's eastern border: after all, China has a stake in the normalization of Russian-EU relations, for though Russia's clashes with the EU have brought China some windfalls (such as lower prices in the 2014 gas deal with Russia), a further worsening of relations between Russia and the EU is not in Beijing's interest. Political instability and conflict are serious challenges to China's BRI, which relies on security and stability. In Eastern Europe, the conflict in Ukraine frustrated some BRI projects; for example, the Chinese project for a deep-sea port in the Crimean peninsula had to be cancelled following the annexation in 2014. It hampered other BRI projects, as well. Nevertheless, China did not openly criticise the annexation of the Crimea – even though Beijing normally champions the principle of non-interference in the national sovereignty of other states, not least because of the five secessionist movements it faces within what it regards as its own borders (Xinjiang, Tibet, Hong Kong, Taiwan and Inner Mongolia). This absence of public criticism by China is telling; it shows that the relationship between China and Russia remains solid, and the EU needs to give this serious thought.

The Authors

Alessia Amighini is Co-Head of Asia Centre and Senior Associate Research Fellow at ISPI. She is Associate Professor of Economics at the Department of Economic and Business Studies (DiSEI) at the University of Piemonte Orientale (Novara, Italy), and Adjunct Professor of International Economics at the Catholic University (Milan, Italy). She previously worked as an Associate Economist at the United Nations Conference on Trade and Development (UNCTAD, Geneva, Switzerland).

Alessandro Arduino is the Co-Director of the International Security & Crisis Management Centre at the Shanghai Academy of Social Sciences (SASS-UNITO) and external affiliate of the Lau China Institute, King's College London. His two decades of experience in China encompass risk analysis and crisis management. His main research interests include the Belt & Road Initiative, security, private military security companies, China's political economy in the MENA region and sovereign wealth funds. He is the author of several books and he has published papers and commentaries in various journals in Italian, English and Chinese. His latest books are: *Securing the Belt and Road Initiative* (2018); *China's Private Army. Protecting the New Silk Road* (2017). He has been made a Knight of the Order of the Italian Star by the President of the Italian Republic.

Aldo Ferrari is Head of the Russia, Caucasus and Central Asia Centre at ISPI. He is Associate Professor of Armenian Language and Culture, History of the Caucasus and Central Asia, and History of the Russian Culture at Ca' Foscari University in Venice, where he is also Director of the ELEO Master's Degree in Languages and Economies of Eastern Europe. Co-founder (2004) and President (2013-2016) of the Association of Italian Studies on Central Asia and the Caucasus (ASIAC), he is Editor of the series "Eurasiatica. Quaderni di studio su Balcani, Iran, Caucaso e Asia Centrale", Ca' Foscari University Press, Venice. Among other publications, he published by ISPI: *Russia 2018. Predictable Elections, Uncertain Future* (2018); *Putin's Russia: Really Back?* (2016); *Beyond Ukraine. EU and Russia in Search of a New Relation* (2015). His main fields of research are Russian History and Culture, Armenian History and Culture, History of the Caucasus, Geopolitics of the Post-Soviet States.

Alexander Gabuev is a Senior Fellow at the Carnegie Moscow Center and Chair of its Russia in the Asia-Pacific Program. His research focuses on Russia's policy towards East and Southeast Asia, political and ideological trends in China, and China's relations with its neighbours, especially those in Central Asia. Before joining Carnegie, he was a member of the editorial board of the Kommersant publishing house and served as Deputy Editor in Chief of Kommersant-Vlast, one of Russia's most influential news weeklies. He has previously been a Non-resident Visiting Research Fellow at the European Council on Foreign Relations (ECFR) and taught courses on Chinese energy policy and political culture at Moscow State University. He is a Munich Young Leader of the Munich International Security Conference and a member of the (Russian) Council on Foreign and Defence Policy.

Vasilii Nosov is an independent expert in the Chinese economy. His research interests focus on the tendencies in China's current economic development, the recent economic policies of the People's Republic of China under the leadership of Xi Jinping, the "bubbles" on China's stock and housing markets, and the developments in the US-China trade war. In 2012-2019, He worked as a Senior Analyst in the Centre for Macroeconomic Research in Sberbank of Russia, the largest bank of Central and Eastern Europe, focusing on the analysis of the Chinese economy and providing regular reports for the bank's top management.

Vita Spivak is currently reading for an MSc in Contemporary Chinese Studies at the University of Oxford, focusing on the development of Sino-Russian relations in the Russian Far East. Before that, she worked from 2015 to 2018 at the Carnegie Moscow Center as Program Coordinator in the Asia-Pacific Program. She regularly contributes to a number of media outlets, mainly on Sino-Russian relations. Her research interests include the contemporary Chinese economy and its foreign direct investment in the energy sector, the anti-corruption campaign in the PRC, and the development of the One Belt, One Road Initiative (OBOR). She has a BA in Chinese History from Moscow State University and an MA in economics from Gubkin Russian State University of Oil and Gas.

Eleonora Tafuro Ambrosetti is a Research Fellow at the Russia, Caucasus and Central Asia Centre at ISPI. Prior to that, she was a Marie Curie Fellow based at the Middle East Technical University (METU) in Ankara, Turkey, where she has also pursued her PhD in International Relations. She has also worked as a junior researcher at the Brussels office of the Foundation for International Relations and Foreign Dialogue (FRIDE) and as a research assistant at the Barcelona Centre for International Affairs (CIDOB). She holds a BA in International Relations from the University of Salento, an MA in European Studies from the University of Roma Tre, and an MRes in International Relations from the Barcelona Institute of International Studies (IBEI). Eleonora's areas of interest include Russia's foreign policy, EU-Russia and Russia-Turkey relations, and EU neighbourhood policies (especially with Eastern neighbours).

www.ingramcontent.com/pod-product-compliance
Lightning Source LLC
Chambersburg PA
CBHW070604050426
42450CB00011B/2978